Series / Number   02-015

A Review of the
Dimensionality of Nations
Project

GORDON HILTON
Northwestern University

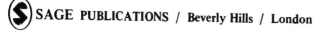

SAGE PUBLICATIONS / **Beverly Hills** / **London**

For information address:

SAGE PUBLICATIONS, INC.
275 South Beverly Drive
Beverly Hills, California 90212

SAGE PUBLICATIONS, INC.
St George's House / 44 Hatton Garden
London EC1N 8ER

International Standard Book Number 0-8039-0224-7

Library of Congress Catalog Card No. L.C. 73-76402

FIRST PRINTING

When citing a professional paper, please use the proper form. Remember to cite the
correct Sage Professional Paper series title and include the paper number. One of the
two following formats can be adapted (depending on the style manual used):

(1) CAPORASO, J. A. (1972) Functionalism and Regional Integration: A Logical
    and Empirical Assessment. Sage Professional Paper in International Studies
    02-004. Beverly Hills and London: Sage Pubns.

OR

(2) Caporaso, James A., *Functionalism and Regional Integration: A Logical and
    Empirical Assessment.* Beverly Hills and London: Sage Professional Paper in
    International Studies 02-004, 1972.

CONTENTS

Introduction 5

Chapter   I. Reviewing DON 6

Chapter II. The History of DON 11

Chapter III. What is DON? 15

Chapter IV. The Needs of International Relations in the
    Early 1960s and the Achievements and
        Strengths of DON 41

Chapter V. Criticisms of DON 46

Chapter VI. Reflections on the Development of DON 67

Notes 71

References 71

Appendix 74

A Review of the Dimensionality of Nations Project

GORDON HILTON
Northwestern University

INTRODUCTION

In the summer of 1972, the Dimensionality of Nations project (DON) completed its tenth year. At that time, as a deliberate policy of R. J. Rummel, the project director, it was reduced in size. Rummel felt that there was a distinct need to distill the various outputs of the project into a cogent, coherent, and comprehensive whole.

As part of this terminating process, I was asked by Professor Rummel to review the work of DON. This I did during the summer of 1971. The result of this was the first version of the DON review (Hilton, 1971), published by the Richardson Institute for Conflict and Peace Research, London. Since then other ideas about DON have occurred to me and, together with suggestions from various readers of the first version, I have produced a much shorter, and I feel better, review.

This second version differs from the previous effort in many ways. There is an extended section on status-field theory and an extra chapter which looks at the development of DON from a history-of-knowledge perspective. These additions have required that I dismiss from the second version much that was in the prior document. For example, a discussion of the achievements of DON in terms of its product, students, and impact on the profession, together with a description of the organization of DON, have been savagely reduced to form Chapter IV here. Previously this had constituted Chapters IV, V, VI, VII, and VIII. Chapter IX, concerned with political implications of DON, has been inserted into Chapter V here, replacing J. E. Vincent's original critique (1972), which has now become available as a DON research report.

Throughout the project, variants of field theory have been produced, mostly by Rummel's students. While I included these in the first version, they are omitted here.

So while much has been left out, I think that other interesting dimensions have been added. Status-field theory, the new research thrust of DON, is given a longer treatment. But more personally interesting (and something I intend to extend in the near future) is the chapter on the development of DON from a history-of-knowledge angle. DON has afforded me the opportunity to use the project as a case study in comparing the various ideas about the growth of knowledge in social science.

Three people have been instrumental in producing this document: R. J. Rummel, the DON Project director, has throughout the whole period been helpful and cooperative in providing much of the evidence upon which the following is based. We have discussed at length both complimentary and critical comments about DON. And I believe that the review is better for this.

Hayward Alker, Jr., read the original version of the review and made many valuable suggestions which have resulted in this improved version.

Linda Radomski edited the first version of the review and, more importantly, has re-edited that version to a size acceptable to the monograph series editor. If there is any coherence contained within the second version it is because of her efforts.

The first version was produced while I was attached to the Richardson Institute for Conflict and Peace Research, London. I thank them for giving me leave of absence to complete the original study.

Finally, the reader who feels a need to go further into the project is encouraged to read the original version of the review and, if still insatiated, read the various outputs from the DON Project which are listed in the Appendix and Reference sections of this paper.

I. REVIEWING DON

With a project as large and complex as DON, there is need for a review from an outside agency. This can be argued for three reasons. First, an external reviewer will presumably have some idea of what he would like to know about the project and in finding this out can make it available for other readers. An internal review would tend to make assumptions about the technical knowledge of the readers; this may mean that some readers would be irretrievably lost from the beginning.

A second advantage of the outside reviewer, although more apparent than real, is that he will preserve objectivity in the assessment of research. An outsider is not involved in the incestuous reinforcement that goes on within large research projects; he is not part of the ethos which argues, "The work we do must be relevant and good because we all believe it to be and we can't all be wrong." However, after constant interaction with the project staff and an increasing awareness of their abilities, the reviewer will eventually suffer with the "it must be right or these intelligent people would not be doing it" syndrome. A further dilution of objectivity will result from the background and interests of the reviewer. He will underline and examine those portions of research which relate specifically to his own competencies, going into these aspects in detail while omitting those which other people might enjoy knowing more about. Overall, an objective reviewer is a myth—the idea just sounds good!

A third advantage is that an external reviewer comments from outside the paradigm of the project. Thus, there will be provided a balance to the various within-paradigm commentaries (Vincent, 1972).

There is no doubt that eventually the best evaluation—in terms of a comprehensive, coherent, and cogent review of the work—will come from the people involved in the project. The project people know best what they set out to do and why, and also to what extent they have succeeded. They know the problems involved more intimately than any outsider ever could. The project staff will produce their "story" of the project. Meanwhile, what follows can be seen as an interim "hors d'oeuvre."

The final judgment of DON, indeed of any comparable exercise, will be some function of the following two factors:

(1) What did the project set out to do and how well did it succeed in these goals?
(2) What is the value of the results as judged by other political scientists?

Basically, all of the important questions will revolve around the total intellectual capital gained during the ten years of the project. Who is prepared to consider it as capital? What contributions in theory, data gathering, and methodology have been made? What is the quality of the people trained on the project and inserted into the general pool of political scientists? The review will confront these questions.

DIFFICULTIES FOR THE REVIEWER AND A STRATEGY

I have briefly expressed some of the difficulties involved in carrying out a review of this nature; there are more. Ideally, an appraisal of this kind of project should be a form of cost-benefit analysis. The cost of the project is reasonably easy to assess, but not so the benefits.

Benefits have a directionality about them. One cannot just list the benefits of the project; one must also ask: benefits to whom? Indeed, the various readers of this review will look for differing qualities in the work of the project. Such a review has to cater to various kinds of audiences. There are the international relations academicians interested in gaining knowledge of international behavior. There are the practitioners of international affairs who want policy guidance. There are the methodologists who are committed to developing better techniques with which to process observations of international behavior. Each of these various audiences will evaluate the work of DON in different ways.

And at the same time, none of them will be able to comprehend all of the various components of a study as large as DON. They will, at best, have only a patchy comprehension of the whole fabric of the study. The consequences of this undoubtedly will be reflected in their assessment of the project value. The reviewer must therefore attempt to consider all of these differing points of view and disparate abilities. The review must contain in specific sections a perspective for each of the various vested interests. As a result, the review may tend to take on a rather superficial appearance.

The time allocated for the review tends to aggravate this superficiality. The review was produced over a four-month period, compared with ten years expended in completing the project. This commits me to operate at a level commensurate with this time ratio. My particular difficulty is intensified by the considerable production from the project. The reader should appreciate that this is not the review of the work of one man, but of a team of men and women which at times has numbered thirty researchers and has never fallen below five. The size of the task can be seen if we take the average number of researchers per year over the ten years as ten: we have one-third of a man-year in which to look at one hundred man-years of research effort. Such a ratio is bound to determine the depth of the review.

Another difficulty is the unstructured nature of the political science discipline. In the physical sciences there are traditions which prescribe the manner in which the discipline should operate. There are various codes of behavior which guide the actions of researchers in the discipline. Such traditions have not been developed with the social sciences.

As a result of this lack of tradition, few reviews of large projects in international relations have been carried out. The only two that are available (Alker and Snyder, 1970; Hilton, 1970) are of the same project—the Stanford study of conflict and integration. Consequently, there is little historic guidance as to which questions the reviewer should ask, which aspects of research are critical, and which queries the discipline in general would like to pose. Asking about the relevance of a project is not enough. Relevant to whom? Relevant to what? Relevant when? There is a need to develop guidelines for assessment of research—a need for some tradition.

So reviewers of political science projects at the moment are, to some extent, pioneers. They are moving into new areas of research and are asking questions that have not been asked before. They are responsible for providing models for subsequent reviewers. Ultimately, these patterns of appraisal will alter the standards of inquiry for the whole field and consequently will influence research on international relations (see Kuhn, 1962). But that is the future; I am still faced with the problem of little guidance in this endeavor. This may in the end produce a blunderbuss attack on DON rather than a carefully executed, clinical analysis.

Given all of these difficulties, the reviewer has certain other restrictions which have to do with his responsibility as a reviewer. Ideally, in an empirical project, the critic should start with the same ground rules as the initial researchers. He should declare his own initial assumptions, provide his own axiomatic structure, collect the necessary data, and test the alternative hypotheses. He should be aware, and take account, of the motivations behind the project conception and the needs of the discipline at the time of conception. Presumably, this would require the same intellectual and financial resources of the original study. But this is the within-paradigm approach. There is also a need to develop a critique from outside the paradigm; to ask whether the chosen paradigm is the most sensible manner in which to proceed.

What then can the reviewer do? The answer lies in the intellectual honesty of the reviewer. His strategy must be to point out clearly the tactics by which he has chosen his positions. He must take particular pains to describe his own interests and the subsequent shallows and depths of his observations. He must try to increase the objectivity of his report by surveying other people within the field. He should attempt to provide a listing of various criticisms of the project, and he should incorporate his own criticisms with these.

Before leaving the difficulties involved in carrying out such an appraisal, I would like to record two difficulties peculiar to DON. The first problem is the wide confusion in the kind of work executed. Some people believe that the work completely centers around factor analysis (or some other spin dryer). Some feel that DON is nothing more than a large data-collecting project. Others, more intimate with the project, feel that there has been a genuine attempt to develop and test theory. Parts of each of these are true, parts are not. An initial task therefore is to acquaint *all* of the audience with the actual research being done on the project. And this task must be accomplished before evaluation can begin.

The second problem is that the project is, without doubt, the most technically complex being carried out in international relations. Consequently, much effort has gone into making this evaluation meaningful to the least sophisticated political scientist.

THE BACKGROUND OF THE REVIEWER

The project personnel felt that the most dispassionate assessment would come from someone outside the American academic system. A further requirement of the reviewer would be competence in handling the technical aspects of the work, such as the heavy reliance on statistical testing in the development of field theory. So that the reader can better assess my qualifications as a reviewer, the following paragraphs are included.

Trained initially in engineering, I stepped from there to social science via operational research. Much of the work that I have done in political science would be described as denoting an interest in statistical methodology. In 1969, I completed work on a critique of the Stanford Studies which gave me experience in this type of large-scale review and provided the basis for my doctoral thesis (Hilton, 1969). Since then my overriding interest has been in the development and testing of various causal models of international relations, attempting to identify weaknesses in various causal inference techniques.

EVIDENCE USED IN THE REVIEW

The review is based upon the following evidence. Four categories were chosen in the belief that they were the most objective that could be employed.

(1) Publications from DON: A total of 63 research reports, 2 sizeable books (one published, one in manuscript form) and 16 printed articles were scrutinized. DON has consistently followed a policy of communicating all of its research, whether empirical or theoretical. This has been done mainly in the form of research reports.

(2) Research staff interviews: Interviews were conducted with a majority of the research staff, past and present. This included all research associates, research students, and research assistants. They were interviewed with regard to their particular research and to obtain their evaluation of the work done on the project.

(3) Letter survey: The first group was a random sample of 100 political scientists taken from the membership list of the American Political Science Association. The second group consisted of 37 senior academicians in international relations. Almost half of these were chosen deliberately because they are not from the quantitative side of the discipline.

(4) Readers' comments: From time to time, various project members have submitted articles, books, and papers to various publishing outlets. The comments of all responsive readers have been sorted to provide a breakdown of these comments.

People who have worked on DON will notice that in this review there is no mention of various side products of the project—for example, research on United Nations voting patterns. This has been done deliberately to avoid the confusion that its inclusion would undoubtedly cause. To some extent this means that most of the review revolves around the work of Rummel, the principal investigator. It follows that much emphasis is placed upon the three phases of his work as I describe them in the section "What Is DON?" Other kinds of research, unless obviously related to field theory, have been excluded from the review.

To be sure, this may under- or overestimate the value of project contributions, but I feel that clarity is especially important with such technical work.

II. THE HISTORY OF DON

During the past nine years, DON has moved from its original venue, Northwestern University, through two other universities to its present home at the University of Hawaii. In an attempt to locate the project in terms of "who was doing what, when, and where," I have prepared the following history of DON. The history is in note form, and it would aid readers considerably if they read the notes while making use of the flow diagram provided (Figure 1). The whole point of this section will be to reduce the confusion caused by the project's changing research environments and different research staff with disparate research backgrounds and interests.

The project was initiated at Northwestern University by Harold

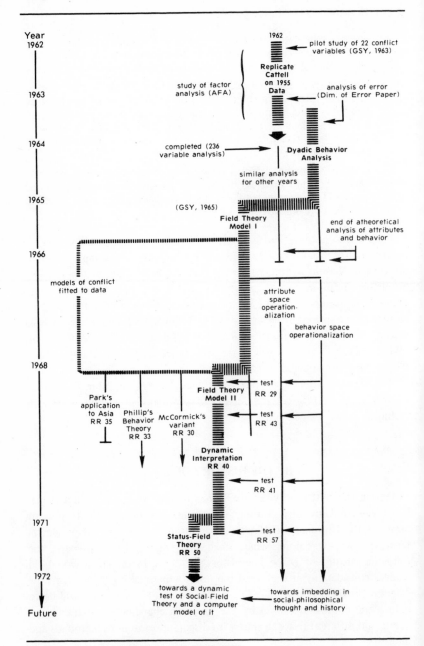

Figure 1: DON RESEARCH FLOW, 1962-1972

Guetzkow, Jack Sawyer, and R. J. Rummel. And although Guetzkow and Sawyer were senior to Rummel, Rummel was de facto project director and has directed the project throughout the whole period.

In the flow diagram used with this section, the prominent thick black line shows the mainline research thrust of the DON project. Some of the personnel listed below were or are concerned with studies not mentioned in the listing. This omission is made to preserve a clarity in demonstrating the incremental research strategy.

1961-1962:

Location:	Northwestern University
Tasks:	Prepare and submit research proposal to National Science Foundation
Personnel:	Guetzkow, Rummel, and Sawyer

1962-1963:

Location:	Northwestern University
Tasks:	(1) replication of Cattell work on attributes of nations
	(2) study of factor analysis technique and operations
	(3) pilot study of 22 conflict variables
	(4) establishment and processing of data error
Personnel:	Harold Guetzkow—principal investigator
	R. J. Rummel—research assistant and de facto director
	Jack Sawyer—technical consultant
	plus three research assistants
Funding Agency:	National Science Foundation

1963-1964:

Location:	Indiana University
Tasks:	(1) complete replication of Cattell work
	(2) begin dyadic analysis of behavior (1955 data)
	(3) begin collection of 1963 data (behavior and attribute)
Personnel:	R. J. Rummel—director and principal investigator
	various research assistants
Funding Agency:	National Science Foundation

1964-1966:

Location:	Yale University
Tasks:	(1) complete dyadic behavior and attribute analysis for 1955 and 1963

(2) design and test various conflict models
(3) develop axiomatic structure of field theory

Personnel:	R. J. Rummel—director and principal investigator Bette Bochelman—computer programmer various faculty; student wives as research assistants
Funding Agency:	National Science Foundation

1966-1968:

Location:	University of Hawaii
Tasks:	(1) operationalize attribute space for test of field theory (2) operationalize behavior space for test of field theory (3) develop field theory
Personnel:	R. J. Rummel—director and principal investigator Steven Brams—research associate Richard Chadwick—research associate Joseph Firestone—research associate Terry Nardin—research associate Michael Shapiro—research associate Charles Wall—computer programmer plus eight research assistants
Funding Agency:	National Science Foundation

1968-1971:

Location:	University of Hawaii
Tasks:	(1) test Models 1 and 2 of field theory (2) test variants of field theory (3) begin collecting data on attribute space for the years 1950, 1960, and 1965 (4) begin the collection of data on behavior space for the years 1950, 1960, and 1965
Personnel:	R. J. Rummel—director Warren Phillips—assistant director Richard Chadwick—research associate Nils Petter Gleditsch—research associate Michael Haas—research associate George Kent—research associate Michael Shapiro—research associate Jack Vincent—research associate Charles Wall—computer programmer plus 19 research assistants and students
Funding Agency:	Advanced Research Projects Agency

1971-1972:

Location:	University of Hawaii
Tasks:	(1) finish data collection for five time points (1950, 1955, 1960, 1963, and 1965)–both attribute and behavior space
	(2) chart the shifts of nations and dyads across attribute and behavior spaces during these time periods
	(3) carry out specific analysis of Asian subset of dyads
	(4) design a computer model of international system based on field theory
	(5) prepare all publications from DON for dissemination among political scientists
	(6) publish all data collected for use in international relations
	(7) design and develop status-field theory
Personnel:	R. J. Rummel–director and principal investigator
	Sang-Woo Rhee–assistant director
	George Kent–research associate
	Charles Wall–computer programmer
	Sumie Ono–data archivist
	plus five research assistants and students
Funding Agency:	Advanced Research Projects Agency

III. WHAT IS DON?

The DON project can be clearly and usefully divided into three segments progressing through time. The initial period (1962-1966) was concerned with the replication of the work of Cattell. During this period, along with the replication, there was a need to familiarize the project personnel with the factor analysis technique. This resulted in the project publication *Applied Factor Analysis* (Rummel, 1970c).

The second period (1964/1965-1971) has revolved around the development and testing of field theory models of international behavior. Throughout this period, realizing that a general theory must demonstrate some facility for encompassing other theories, the project has tried to incorporate Rosenau's (1966) linkage theory, the distance theory of Quincy Wright (1955), and the social status theory of Johan Galtung (1964). Such imbedding has resulted in the conception of status-field theory. A description of this latest axiomatic structure has recently appeared (Rummel, 1971), and its development and testing will be carried out during the third period, which began in 1971.

What follows is a description of each of the three periods and the ideas generated therein. I shall attempt to explain in a nontechnical manner all of the developments in each of the periods, particularly the axioms upon which field theory and to a large extent, status-field theory are based.

The final piece in this section will distinguish between the various theories produced on the project and the use of the factor analysis technique. It is a truism that the terms "DON Project" and "factor analysis" have been used almost interchangeably. Reasons for this are given where the publication difficulties are discussed. Nevertheless, a clarification should be made.

The reader may find it useful to refer occasionally to the earlier flow chart (Figure 1).

ATHEORETICAL BEGINNINGS

Much of the contemporary criticism of DON alleges that the research thrust revolved around an atheoretical, inductive approach to the analysis of international relations. To some extent this is a fair judgment *if* based upon the output from the work of the project during the years 1962-1966. And though the major research thrust since 1965 has been field theory, these criticisms are still made. The fault here may lie in the sluggishness with which research is communicated. There is a slowness in the preparation of manuscripts coupled with a reluctance on the part of some journals to publish the work. All of this has been aggravated by the long publication waiting lists once a publication has been accepted. For example, the work carried out during 1962-1966 has existed in manuscript form since 1967-1968. It remained unpublished until late 1972. However, one cannot deny that there was much inductive "number-crunching" in the initial years of the project. Similarly, one must also acknowledge that any rigorous testing of field theory may not have been possible without these preliminary excursions with data.

The motivation for the activity during these three years stems from two of the people initially involved. On one hand, Harold Guetzkow felt that there was a lack of soundly collected cross-national data and tested propositions. Such data, if they were to become available, would be helpful in providing the solid information that he needed to validate his simulation models. On the other hand, Jack Sawyer had read the work of Raymond Cattell (and Gorsuch, 1965) and had felt that there was a need for replication of his study using more modern data. However, neither was able to carry out such a study full time, and so Rummel was incorporated into the project and became de facto project leader.

Throughout the four years that followed, five major functions were carried out. All of these functions were vital to the testing of field theory which followed this initial work.

Collection of the 1955 attribute data (Rummel, 1972): In order to determine the main dimensions of attribute space, the initial job was to collect data on all the various nation attributes for the period selected. A list of 600 possibilities for inclusion were culled from various studies in international relations. Since this number exceeded the capacity of the available computer, the number of variables was finally reduced to 230. The pruning was done by Sawyer, Guetzkow, and Rummel, using criteria such as the catholicity and theoretical or policy relevance of each variable. The year 1955 was chosen because it was the latest available datum at that time.

Previously, decisions had been made as to which nations to include in the analysis. The criteria for this selection were: (1) nations with a population of over 800,000, and (2) nations that were neither colonies, protectorates, nor territories. Under these criteria, 82 nations qualified.

Data were collected mainly from the *United Nations Statistical Yearbook, Demographic Yearbook* and *World Social Situation.* Other sources used less often were: UNESCO's *Facts and Figures,* Ginsberg's *Atlas of Economic Development,* and the *New York Times.*

Errors and Omissions in the data (Rummel and Wall, 1969): Two major error possibilities were present. The first was error produced by the collectors and punchcard operators on DON. This was reduced, to a large extent, by the checking procedures within the project itself. The second type of error was imbedded within the data before they came to the project—for example, error in the data collected by the United Nations. Missing data were a particularly severe problem since they amounted to something like 17% of the total. Rummel and Wall provided a technique for estimating the missing data from the data present; they also discussed possible effects of this technique on the results.

Production of the attribute dimensions (Rummel, 1972): Obviously, an 82 by 236 cell matrix is of limited use. Having prepared the data, the next step was to reduce the data into something manageable, but without any loss of basic information. The technique employed for this reduction was factor analysis.

Later in this section there is some attempt to place this technique in its relationship to field theory. The basic argument is that factor analysis distills the data—both attribute and behavior—into the two Euclidean spaces upon which field theory is founded. It is a method by which the raw data are "converted" into data that are relevant to the theory as presented. However, in the earlier period of DON, it was used as a reduction technique, and its use explained as such:

> What Factor Analysis does is this. It takes thousands and potentially millions of measurements and qualitative observations and resolves them into their distinct patterns of occurrence [Rummel, 1967b: 445].

With some notable exceptions, this has had much to do with the way that Rummel's work on field theory has been judged by his contemporaries. The belief is that this is *all* that factor analysis can do; many are unaware that it can operationalize particular theories based on Euclidean space. Their acceptance of Rummel's subsequent work on field theory has been jaundiced by this unawareness.

Initially, the factor analysis procedure was used solely as an ordering device for the mass of data collected. This ordering produced 15 different dimensions around which almost 80% of the total data clustered (Rummel, 1972). This meant that all of the 236 variables could be reduced to 15 dimensions (or dimensions in attribute space) with a loss of just over 20% of the data. Further, it was found that 3 of these dimensions—economic development, size, and political orientation—account for over 40% of the information in the original matrix. Other major dimensions were: Catholic culture, foreign conflict behavior, density (population per square mile), and domestic conflict behavior. Each nation was ranked in terms of factor scores on these dimensions of attribute space.

Relationships between attributes and behavior: Among the 236 variables included in the attribute space, there were 89 total-behavior variables. Before we move on to the next section which describes the dyadic behavioral variable, it would seem wise to distinguish between this total-behavior variable included in attribute space and the dyadic behavior variable. Dyadic behavior is individual in the sense that it is the behavior of one nation towards another specified nation. The total-behavior data included in the attribute space are accumulated incidences of this behavior over the time period; although the actor-nation is defined, the object-nation is not. An example of the behavior in attribute data would be the total number of public demonstrations toward foreign nations; while in the dyadic variable, it would be the total number of public demonstrations by one actor-nation towards a particular specified object-nation. The behavior in attribute data denotes a propensity of that nation toward a certain kind of behavior, such as threats. It is a descriptor of that nation, as is GNP or population size. The difference between the two types of behavior variable is definitional.

Returning to the attribute space, with its included total-behavior variables, an attempt was made to locate nations on the dimensions of international behavior. In the same way that nations could be placed on the 15 dimensions of attribute space, so too could they be placed on the dimensions of a behavior space which included a foreign conflict behavior dimension, an aid dimension, an ideology dimension, and a popularity dimension. The relationship between attributes and this nondirectional behavior was tested through 11 hypotheses, listed elsewhere (Rummel, 1972). Briefly, each was designed to test some relationship between attributes and international behavior—for example, the hypothesis that foreign conflict behavior is related to the level of economic or technological development of a nation. The testing showed that conflict behavior is little related to attributes.

Collection of dyadic behavior data (Rummel, 1968): The dyadic data collection was accomplished in the same systematic fashion as the collection of attribute data. It did not prove possible to collect data on all of the dyads produced by the 82 original nations; this would have meant over 3,000 of them. Instead, 166 were chosen randomly and, as a check of these, others were selected. For each of these dyads (and remember that the behavior dyad "US→China" is distinct from that of "China→US") data were collected on 153 variables for the year 1955. Factor analysis of these data produced the dyadic behavior space upon which all dyads can be located.

Very little analysis of these dimensions of behavior space was carried out, as the project's major research thrust at this point was to test field theory. Thus, much attention was given to the relationship between the two Euclidean spaces, attribute and behavior, produced from a factor analysis of the data.

The development and testing of field theory is described in the following section. Since the collection of the data for the year 1955, the same techniques of data collection—e.g., coding, sources, and so forth—have been used to produce data for attribute (A-space) and dyadic behavior space (B-space) for the years 1963, 1950, 1960, and 1965. Eventually, these will allow a dynamic test of field theory.

FIELD THEORY

As we saw in the previous section, much of the work of the initial period on DON attempted the identification of the two spaces, attribute space (A-space) and behavior space (B-space). There had been little effort to link these two spaces in a theoretical fashion. On one hand, there was A-space, a Euclidean space with attribute dimensions within which each nation could be located. It was relatively easy to gauge the distances between nations on the various attribute dimensions. On the other hand, there was B-space, another Euclidean space with behavior dimensions upon which each nation dyad could be located. Therefore, the behavior of nation X toward nation Y (a dyad) and the behavior of Y toward X (a different dyad) could be located in this space. The basic theory, field theory, linked the nature of a nation (attributes) to the behavior of that nation. The theory holds that the distance between nations in attribute space provides the social force which determines the behavior of one nation to the other. In this way, attribute space is linked to behavior space.

In the very early period of the project, the staff, while working on the theory, was committed to completing the atheoretical analyses of data described in the previous section. The two operations were carried on simultaneously, and this may have produced the confusion about the work of DON that still persists. To the casual onlooker, it seemed that no fundamental change took place at that time; and since the project had been involved with atheoretical number-crunching, this was assumed to be the continuing research direction. This is not the case. From the parturition of field theory, except for the commitment to finishing the data collection already begun in 1963-1964, the whole research thrust has been toward developing and testing field theory.

Field theory is based upon seven axioms. The first four of the axioms are broadly definitional and have hardly changed in wording over the eight years; the other three have contained the testable portion of the theory and have been altered as intuition and testing dictated. These particular axioms have been changed quite considerably; indeed, one was found to be redundant and has been eliminated. It should be pointed out that in the original exposition of these axioms (Rummel, 1965a: 183) they were described as "theoretical statements." Their promotion to "axioms" has eliminated much logical vagueness in the framework. Rummel points this out with the qualification that "they functioned as axioms in the theoretical development and I thought of them as such" (Rummel, 1969b: 10).

There is no logical inconsistency here. They are axioms inasmuch as: (1) they are consistent—i.e., neither they nor any theorem deducible from them contradicts one another; (2) they are complete—i.e., they adequately encompass this particular portrayal of "reality;" and (3) there is no redundancy—i.e., they are independent of one another and no one can be deduced from any other. The initial description of them as theoretical propositions was partially incorrect and possibly based upon timidity on the part of Rummel.

In the following pages, I will state each of these axioms and consider their implications for the theory. Those axioms that have been changed or eliminated will be discussed more fully, and some attempt will be made to describe the reasoning behind the revisions.

> *Axiom 1.* International relations is a field consisting of all the attributes and interactions of nations and their complex interrelationships.

Attributes are defined as any description of that nation that is capable of differentiating it from another nation. For example, gross national product, number of cars per family, birth rate, death rate, and so on. It is possible to develop a whole series of such descriptors and to collect data for each nation on them.

Interaction between nations is a behavioral act, the basic deliberation being: who did what and to whom. This locates the behavioral act in terms of the actor-nation and the object-nation. This is the dyad. The "what" is the behavioral act. And in the same way that nations can be positioned in attribute space by their attributes, so can dyads in behavior space by their behavior. The dyad also imparts direction to the behavioral act. The dyad US→UK is different from the dyad UK→US; this difference is as fundamental in behavior space as the difference between each nation in attribute space.

> *Axiom 2.* The international field can be analytically divided into attribute and behavior spaces wherein attributes and interactions are projected, respectively, as vectors.

This axiom places the whole framework of the project within linear mathematics by stating that the international field can be thought of in terms of space. More fundamentally, such an axiom assures the theory of one operational means for testing. This axiom allows the use of such techniques as canonical analysis, multiple regression, and factor analysis.

Axiom 3. The attribute and behavior spaces are generated by a finite
set of linearly independent dimensions.

If there were an infinite set of dimensions in either attribute or
behavior space, the theory would be untestable. Any refutation of the
theory could be countered by arguing the infinite nature of each space. By
this axiom, space is defined as finite. Each of the spaces contains not only
specific dimensions—such as area, national income, and so forth (attributes) or exports, threats, and so forth (behavior)—but all the linear
combinations of these dimensions. This is where factor analysis comes into
its own. From the myriad of information of N nations with M attributes,
factor analysis produces a few basic dimensions (called factors) and locates
each of the nations in space without discarding much of the original
information. It performs in a similar fashion for behavior space.

Axiom 4. Nations are located as vectors in attribute space and coupled
as dyads in behavior space.

As we saw in an earlier section, attributes and behavior can be thought
of as the dimensions of two spaces which enable the location of nations
and dyads. Let us take a two-dimensional example and consider the
distance between two major cities, Chicago and Miami. The location of
Chicago in this two-dimensional space is Y miles north of Miami on a
north-south dimension and X miles west of Miami on an east-west
dimension. This location is precise on these two axes. Suppose, however,
we inserted another axis which enabled us to determine say, the difference
in heights between various buildings in the two cities. We are now able to
locate in this three-dimensional space every point on every building in
Chicago in terms of distance along the N-S dimensions from Miami, its
distance along the E-W dimension from Miami and also its distance in
height from a given point in Miami. Attribute and behavior spaces are
conceptually similar. In attribute space, the coordinates are the attributes
and nations are located in this space; in behavior space, the behavior
dimensions are the coordinates while the dyads are located in this space.
The location takes the form of a vector which indicates the length and
direction of the nation or dyad, in attribute or behavior space respectively,
from the origin of the space. The origin of the space is the point at which
all of the dimensions of that space intersect.

The ability to understand this is impaired by human inability to
imagine more than three or four axes in Euclidean space. For example,
when space is three-dimensional as in the Miami-Chicago example it is
relatively easy to comprehend. However, when we move into spaces of

four or more dimensions, as are attribute and behavior spaces, then difficulties arise. The reader will find it helpful to remember that whatever holds in the two- and three-dimensional cases also holds in n-dimensional cases. The only difficulty is that the human mind cannot picture this; fortunately, mathematics can cope with it.

Axioms 1 to 4 have been relatively constant over the whole period of development and can be identified as the hard inner core of field theory.

Axiom 5. Distance vectors in A-space (attribute space) that connect nations are *social forces* determining the location of dyads in B-space (behavior space).

The axiom states simply that the distance between two nations in A-space will produce (cause or determine) the behavior of these nations towards each other. Except in special and nontestable circumstances, this relationship between attributes and behavior is asymmetric. We shall discuss this more fully when we consider Axiom 7.

The term "distance vector" can be more easily explained if we return to our Miami-Chicago example. As we saw earlier, using Miami as the origin of our coordinate system, it is possible to locate Chicago in this coordinate space. In the same way, it is possible to locate, say, New York. Having done this, the position of New York relative to Chicago can also be imagined and computed still using Miami as the origin. The line from Chicago to New York will also have a length and a direction and is therefore a vector.

Returning to A-space, we saw that nations can be located in this space. So if we consider two nations located somewhere in this attribute space, we can imagine a line between them which is called an attribute distance vector. It is this distance vector that provides the social force which determines the behavior of the actor-nation toward the object-nation and the location of the dyad in behavior space.

This axiom allows the following equation which is called Model 1.

$$w_{i \to j,k} = \alpha_1 d_{i \to j,1} + \alpha_2 d_{i \to j,2} + \dots + \alpha_p d_{i \to j,p} \qquad \text{[Model 1]}$$

This equation states that the behavior of nation i toward nation j on behavior dimension k, $w_{i \to j,k}$ is a linear addition of the distance vectors between i and j on all of the attribute dimensions, where there are a total of p such dimensions. The parameters α_1, α_2, and so forth, describe mathematically the precise relationship between $w_{i \to j,k}$ and $d_{i \to j,1}$, $d_{i \to j,2}$, and so on. Again, an example: suppose there are just two attribute dimensions which we call power and economic development. In this attribute space, we can locate all nations. Suppose further we are interested in the behavior dimension conflict. That is, we imagine only one behavior dimension. In addition, we may be mostly interested in the dyad US → China. The equation could now be stated as:

$$w_{US \to China, conflict} = \alpha_{power} d_{US \to China, power} + \alpha_{ec.dev.} d_{US \to China, ec.dev.}$$

Obviously, this example is not realistic, since the behavior of the United States toward China will depend upon many more attribute dimensions and will be manifest in many more ways than by conflict alone.

However, this is testable. As we saw earlier, both attribute and behavior spaces can be extracted from the data. Consequently, nations and dyads can be located precisely in attribute and behavior space respectively. Thus, we can obtain a value $w_{US \to China, conflict}$ and we can compute the vector distances $d_{US \to China, power}$ and $d_{US \to China, ec.dev.}$, and with these test the validity of the theoretical relationship for various time periods.

Model 1 described a need for the operationalization of both attribute and behavior space. This operationalization was achieved over the years 1966-1968. Meanwhile, the model had come under some criticism from a student involved in the project. He pointed out the difficulty of using symmetric parameters: such symmetry would predict that the behavior of one nation in a dyad toward another would be exactly the reverse of the behavior of that nation toward the original nation. This is because the parameter on any attribute dimension is conceived of as constant across sets of nations. Suppose we are considering the attribute "power" and find that the United States on this attribute is 3 while the United Kingdom is 1. The attribute distance vector for the dyad US → UK is therefore +2 and the behavior will be some function of $+2\alpha_{power}$. However, if we reverse the dyad and compute the behavior of the United Kingdom toward the United States, our attribute distance is now 1 minus 3 and the behavior will be some function of $-2\alpha_{power}$. The model would therefore predict exactly opposite behavior, signified by the change of the sign from plus to minus. This is in fact a "turning the other cheek" theory and therefore not entirely in accord with one's experience of international relations. As an example, suppose the United States imposed tariffs upon United Kingdom goods imported into the States. The model would predict that the United Kingdom would, at the same time, not only drop all its import tariffs on

United States goods, but positively encourage the sale of United States goods in the United Kingdom!

As a result of this criticism, a competing model was developed. This model linked the parameter to the acting nation in the dyad. In this way, the behavior of one nation to another is unlikely to have the symmetric aspect predicted in Model 1, although Model 2 still allows this. That is, symmetry is *allowed for* in Model 2, whereas this was assumed in Model 1. In equation form, Model 2 is;

$$w_{i \rightarrow j,k} = \alpha_{i,1} d_{i \rightarrow j,1} + \alpha_{i,2} d_{i \rightarrow j,2} + \ldots + \alpha_{i,p} d_{i \rightarrow j,p} \qquad \text{[Model 2]}$$

We can again use the US → China example. Interpreting this equation to predict conflict behavior as a function of the differences between the two attributes of power and economic development, we get;

$$w_{US \rightarrow China, conflict} = \alpha_{US,power} d_{US \rightarrow China, power} +$$
$$\alpha_{US,ec.dev.} d_{US \rightarrow China, ec.dev.}$$

Looking back to the equation produced by Model 1 and this example, we see that in Model 2, as distinct from Model 1, the fundamental difference is in the parameter

$$w_{US \rightarrow China, conflict} = \alpha_{power} d_{US \rightarrow China, power} +$$
$$\alpha_{ec.dev.} d_{US \rightarrow China, ec.dev.}$$

In Model 1, α_{power} and $\alpha_{ec.dev.}$ are not tied to any state and are thus constant across all nations. In Model 2 these parameters are tied to the actor-nation. The change from Model 1 to Model 2 results in some loss in generality.

Four tests of the models have now been completed (Rummel, 1969b; Rummel and Van Atta, 1970; Rummel, 1970a, 1965b: 131; Rhee, 1971) although other "heuristic" treatments (Park, 1969) and comparative tests (Gleditsch, 1970) had been carried out previously. The four major empirical tests of the models have supported Model 2. In Research Report 29 (see Appendix for listing of DON research reports), both models were tested using 1955 data. Model 1 fitted the data poorly, while Model 2 fitted very well. A replication of this test using 1963 data was carried out in Research Report 43. In this test, Model 1 failed ignominiously, while Model 2 again fit the data well. It was after this test that Model 1 was superseded by Model 2. Both Research Reports 41 and 57 tested Model 2 for a reduced set of actors (and therefore dyads), the results remained consistently good.

> *Axiom 6.* The direction and velocity of movement over time of a dyad in behavior space is along the resolution vectors of the forces.

We have seen that as attribute distance vectors between nations change, so will their behavior towards one another. However, this does not identify the time at which the causal influence operates. Do attribute distances in the previous time segment $(t - 1)$ lead to behavior in this time period (t), or do the forces act simultaneously? As attributes change, does behavior change too?

This axiom specifies that the link between attributes and behavior is instantaneous. Also, behavior is not linked either directly or indirectly with either previous attribute differences or previous behaviors. Other theories, offshoots of field theory, have been suggested and tested (McCormick, 1969; Phillips, 1970) but the mainline research has prescribed instantaneity between cause (attribute difference) and effect (behavior).

Nevertheless, there are some strong assumptions involved in adopting this axiom, and this led to a research report concerned solely with this axiom (Rummel, 1970b). The ideas contained in this article are particularly difficult to visualize. Basically, it argues that the inclusion of time as a dimension in attribute space makes it possible to relate a nation's attributes to this time vector. The result of this projection is a "social time" in which nations at the same calendar time can be conceived of as moving at different speeds along a particular attribute dimension, much in the way that two cars on the same road (dimension) can, at any instant in calendar time, be moving at different speeds.

Although other aspects of time will be discussed, particularly when we discuss causal problems of the model, the work involved in the "Social Time ..." paper has made the original Axiom 6 redundant, and it has now been dropped.

> *Axiom 7.* Behavior space is a subspace of attribute space.

This particular axiom is not derived from a philosophical premise; it is provided for mathematical convenience. We saw in Axiom 5 that distances between attributes provide the social force causing behavior. For this to be mathematically consistent, the behavior space must contain less than or as many dimensions as the attribute space. An example will illustrate this.

Consider the relationship between a table top surface (two-dimensional) and a room in which the table top surface is located (three-dimensional). While one can locate the table top surface accurately in the room (i.e., location from three to two dimensions), one cannot locate the room from the table top surface (location from two to three dimensions).

This does not, however, mean that the theory embodied in Axiom 5 is tautological. It is true, as I have said, that if behavior space is smaller than attribute space, this will determine the mathematical causal direction in the model. But whether, in reality, the number of dimensions of behavior is less than the number of attribute dimensions can be tested empirically. Data can be collected on all attributes and on all the behaviors. Analysis of these will produce the basic dimensions of each space. These can readily be counted and compared. Intuitively, however, it would be reasonable to expect more attribute than behavior dimensions.

This completes the review of the axiomatic structure of field theory. In my discussion of the axioms, I hope that I have encouraged a realization that theory has been the main objective of research from 1965-1971. The axiomatic structure can be divided into two sections: the first four are analytical axioms which gradually bring the structure to a point where it is possible to test the empirical axioms—5, 6, and 7. As we shall see in . Chapter VI, this division also separates what I have called the hard inner core of the theory (Axioms 1,2,3, and 4) from the protective belt of middle range hypotheses and models (Axioms 5, 6, and 7).

To some extent testing has been carried out, although Axiom 5 has been subjected to more testing than 6 and 7, and 6 has suffered complete elimination. Axiom 7, which is as fundamental to field theory as any of the others, has been neglected.

STATUS-FIELD THEORY

One of the characteristics of a good theoretical structure is its ability to incorporate existing knowledge. The more theories it subsumes, the greater claims can be made regarding its generality. This realization has encouraged those involved in DON to generalize field theory by embodying within it previous theories of international behavior.

An initial attempt at this was an analysis called "United States Foreign Relations: Conflict, Cooperation and Attribute Differences." (Rummel, 1970a). The document reported the testing of propositions derived from different theories about international behavior. The criterion used was their individual ability to predict the international behavior of the United States. Propositions were derived from the following theories:

Rummel's field theory

Rosenau's "pre-theory" (Rosenau, 1966)

Wright's distance theory (Wright, 1955)

Galtung's status theory (Galtung, 1964)

Organski's power theory (Organski, 1960)

Geographical distance theory

Field theory and parts of status theory were found to be the most powerful predictors of the international behavior of the United States. This has lead to an attempt on the part of the principal investigator on the project to develop an axiomatic structure which couples field theory and status theory. In the same way that DON changed fundamentally from atheoretical beginnings to mainline research on field theory, there has been this further change to status-field theory (see Figure 1).

Status-field theory is, at once, a more substantively opulent theoretical structure than field theory. In Rummel's introduction to the seminal piece on the hybrid theory, he points out,

> Field Theory has an explicit axiomatic and mathematical structure specifying the form of relationship between international behavior and attribute distances, but not the direction of the relationship. That is, although postulating how behavior links to attribute distances, Field Theory does not indicate which specific behavior is a consequence of particular positive or negative attribute distances. Field Theory therefore appears as a mathematical skeleton, some-what barren of substantive meaning and implications.

> By contrast, status theory seems substantively rich in application. Behavior's correlation with status is often specified, enabling theoretical discussion of specific international questions such as East-West summitry or disputes before the International Court of Justice. Although the axiomatic base is given, it is not articulated within a mathematical system; the functional relationship between status measures and interactions is not given. Consequently, status theory cannot easily be treated deductively.

> A natural question is then whether field theory and status theory can be unified. Since the "failings" of each are apparently the strengths of the other, combining them would make a better theory of international relations. This paper will show that there is a positive answer and that the two can be united by imbedding status theory in field theory's mathematical structure: status theory will be a special case of field theory [Rummel, 1971].

Thus, status theory is subsumed under field theory and the resulting cross-breed consists of nine axioms; three taken from field theory and the rest from status theory. We can look at these in order and point out differences from the original field theory. At the same time various derived theorems, corollaries, and definitions will be discussed.

Status-Field Space

> *Axiom 1 (Status Field Axiom).* International relations is a field consisting of all nation attributes and interactions and their complex relationship through time.

This axiom is almost the same as the first one of field theory, the only difference being the addition of the term "through time." The change results from the work completed on the time aspect of field theory (Rummel, 1970b).

> *Axiom 2 (Attribute Behavior Space Axiom).* The international field comprises a Euclidean attribute space defining all nation attributes and a Euclidean behavior space defining all nation dyadic interactions.

Presumably, this single axiom replaces Axioms 2, 3 and 4 of the original field theory axioms. The first theorem is derived from this axiom.

> *Theorem 1 (Finite Dimensionality Theorem).* A finite set of linearly independent dimensions generate attribute and behavior space.

This theorem has close resemblance to Axiom 3 of the original field theory. It suggests that a finite number of dimensions encapsulate all the independent nation variation on an infinite number of attributes. The theorem operates in a similar fashion for behavior space.

> *Axiom 3 (Stratification Axiom).* International relations is a stratified social system.

Here then we have the first of the status axioms. It likens the international system to a social system of which one characteristic is some form of ranking of its members—a plausible suggestion. This axiom generates a second theorem.

> *Theorem 2 (Status Theorem).* Status dimensions are a subset of attribute dimensions.

The proposal here is that status dimensions are really clusters of nation attributes by which a nation is ranked on some continuum. For example, we may rank nations on wealth, an attribute dimension consisting of such components as GNP per capita, telephones per capita, and so on. In addition, this theorem allows the total number of status dimensions to be less than the number of attribute dimensions.

Incorporated at this point are two definitions which (1) insert the idea of desire or motivation by a nation to achieve high as against low status, and (2) recognize only the status dimensions of economic development and power. Rummel (1971) suggests that there is much evidence to support these definitions. *Corollary 1* also appears, proposing: Status is a continuous variable.

Theorem 3 (Position Theorem). Nations are located as vectors in attribute space and as vectors of nation dyads in behavior space.

This theorem is similar in wording to Axiom 4 of the original field theory. Provision is made for the positioning of nations in attribute space and nation dyads in behavior space. This now allows the incorporation of the proposition *(Corollary 2)* that an attribute space position defines a nation's relative status.

Theorem 4 (Mobility Theorem). Nations desire upward status mobility.

This theorem can be put forward by the implication of an earlier definition that there is a desire or motivation by a nation to achieve high as against low status. Not implied by any definition so far is Theorem 5.

Theorem 5 (Equilibration Theorem). Nations having unbalanced statuses desire to balance them.

To clarify all of this, let us consider nations with either high status T or low status U. Given there are only two status dimensions, economic development and power, the following four possibilities occur for any nation; TT, TU, UT, UU, where a nation with the status designation TT is high on both economic development and power, a nation with the status designation TU is high on economic development but low on power. While TT and UU are status-balanced, TU and UT are not. The equilibration theorem predicts that nations with unbalanced status would desire to balance their status on these dimensions. The mobility theorem would predict that this would be achieved not by reducing the Ts to Us but by increasing the Us to Ts. The reader should bear in mind that although I have used only a dichotomous variable in this example, the status dimensions allow a continuous scaling as per Corollary 1.

Having humanized the nation entity by stating that it "desires," Rummel now adds the following third corollary. The *elite corollary* states: A nation's elite identify with their rank and status configuration. This corollary enables the application of individual-level sociological propositions at the nation level. Thus officials at the center of a national society and having high all-around status will conduct foreign relations according to the status of their nation.

We now come to perhaps the central definition in the whole structure. The reader will remember there are only two status dimensions. These are economic development and power (by previous definition). Delineating the rank of a nation therefore will necessitate a combination of the position of that nation on each of these dimensions. The rank definition formalized this.

> *Rank Definition.* The rank of nation i is $\alpha_1 s_{i1} + \alpha_2 s_{i2}$, where α_1 and α_2 are positive parameters and s_{i1} and s_{i2} are nation i's economic development and power statuses, respectively.

Thus the rank of any nation is some weighted addition of their position on both of the status dimensions. Let me use a more tangible example. Suppose the nation is the United States; the rank of the United States would be represented by:

$$\alpha_{ec.dev.} status_{US,ec.dev.} + \alpha_{power} status_{US,power}$$

where $\alpha_{ec.dev.}$ is a positive parameter individual to economic development and α_{power} is another positive parameter individual to power. $Status_{US,ec.dev.}$ and $status_{US,power}$ are respectively the position of the United States on the economic development and power status dimensions. Thus, the rank of a nation is a weighted sum of these two status positions.

But this is for a single nation. It may be that we would want to test hypotheses concerning the joint rank of two nations. For example, the higher the combined rank of two nations, the less likely they are to exhibit conflict behavior toward one another. This, together with the important point that we are dealing with behavior dyads, provides a need for a joint rank definition:

> *Joint Rank Definition.* The joint rank of two nations, i and j, is $\alpha_1(s_{i1} + s_{j1}) + \alpha_2(s_{i2} + s_{j2})$, where α_1 and α_2 are the same parameters as in the rank definition.

For example, the joint rank of the United States and China would be represented by:

$$\alpha_{ec.dev.} \text{ (combined status of the United States and China}$$
$$\text{on the ec. dev. dimension)} +$$
$$\alpha_{power} \text{ (combined status of the United States and China}$$
$$\text{on the power dimension)}$$

Verbally, this is a weighted sum of the addition of both nations' positions on the two status dimensions, economic development and power.

Earlier, it was emphasized in the equilibration theorem that nations having unbalanced statuses desire to remedy this. Obviously this generates a need for a measure of status disequilibrium.

Status Disequilibrium Definition. A nation's status disequilibrium is $\pm\alpha_1 s_{i1} \pm \alpha_2 s_{i2}$ where α_1 and α_2 have different signs.

This definition is expressed in what might seem an unusually complex way to enable discrimination in the case where one nation's status is symbolized as UT, and the other's status as TU. Absolute differences, used as a measure of disequilibrium, would produce exactly the same measure, despite the manifest differences in the situation. As Rummel argues,

> Considering the first status as achieved (economic development) and the second as ascribed (power), then TU and UT statuses will not equally affect behavior. The frustrations and psychological stress of the black doctor with high achievement and low ascribed status (race) will be different in nature and intensity than the white laborer's [Rummel, 1971: 44].

One also needs some measure of status disequilibrium between the dyad of nations, one of the theory's basic entities. This is given by the status incongruence definition.

Status Incongruence Definition. The status incongruence of two nations i and j is $\pm\alpha_1(s_{i1} - s_{j1}) \pm \alpha_2(s_{i2} - s_{j2})$, where α_1 and α_2 have different signs.

As with the joint rank definition and rank definition, the status incongruence function is the summation of two individual nations' status disequilibrium functions. The reader should substitute United States for i, China for j, economic development status for 1 and power status for 2, as done previously. This might lead to a more substantive understanding of the symbols.

Returning now to the link between attribute space and status, the status distance corollary states:

> *Status Distance Corollary.* Status incongruence between nations i and j is the distance vector between their status vectors on a status dimension.

Simply, this inserts status incongruence of any dyad into the formal Euclidean attribute space. It links the attribute distance notion of field theory to the concept of status distance (status incongruence).

Finally, in this subsection of status field theory called status-field space, there is the fundamental behavior-attribute linkage which will enable not only the incorporation of the original field theory idea that attribute distance causes behavior, but also that a subset of attribute distance—status distance (or incongruence)—causes behavior. The linkage is formally presented as follows.

> *Axiom 4 (Attribute Distance Axiom).* Between nation attribute distances at a particular time are social forces determining dyadic behavior at that time.

This is similar in content to Axiom 5 of field theory with the added qualifications concerning time. Such qualifications were enforced by the "Social Time . . . " paper (Rummel, 1970b).

In field theory, two models were derived from this axiom. As we have seen, one of them, Model 1, did not test well and has been replaced by Model 2. Status-field theory is therefore limited to Model 2.

So far status-field theory attempts to place two status dimensions in attribute space. These status dimensions are economic development and power. It has also proposed various nation motivations created by status positions. It went further to operationalize various measures of status disequilibrium and rank disequilibrium, which would facilitate some testing of the various theorems and their corollaries. And finally it inserted all of this in attribute space, thus providing a field theoretic framework for the influence of status on behavior. There has, as yet, been no discussion of any relationship between the attributes and their subset statuses on behavior. This follows in the next section.

Rank and Behavior

> *Axiom 5 (Status Dependence Axiom).* Some behavior dimensions are linearly dependent on status.

This formalizes status theory's fundamental notion that status explains behavior. Since we have seen that status dimensions are a subset of attribute dimensions and similarly that attribute distances cause behavior, this axiom provides the formal link between behavior and status.

The axiom also enables two further definitions. The first, status role definition, stipulates that the status dependent behavior dimensions define a nation's role. The second, status behavior definition, clarifies "status behavior" by asserting that the status dependent behavior dimensions delineate status behavior.

> *Axiom 6 (Rank Behavior Axiom).* Status behavior is directed toward higher ranking nations and the greater a nation's rank, the more its status behavior.

Thus, if trade were a status behavior, the higher status nations would trade more.

> *Axiom 7 (Status Quo Axiom).* High ranking nations support the current international order.

Nations high on economic development and power not only have wealth, but also have an ability to increase and protect their wealth with considerable power. These last two axioms together suggest that nations high in status will have much interaction and be very cooperative with each other (particularly concerning threats to the status quo). The two axioms lead to the important cooperation theorem:

> *Theorem 6 (Cooperation Theorem).* The higher the joint rank of nations i and j the more cooperative their behavior.

This is expressed more formally as: $CO_{i \to j} = -\alpha_{i1} d_{i-j,1} - \alpha_{i2} d_{i-j,2}$, where $CO_{i \to j}$ is a behavior cluster of highly intercorrelated cooperation vectors, and $d_{i-j,1} = s_{i1} - s_{j1}$. Similarly, $d_{i-j,2} = s_{i2} - s_{j2}$. In substituting, $CO_{i \to j} = -\alpha_{i1}(s_{i1} - s_{j1}) - \alpha_{i2}(s_{i2} - s_{j2})$. Obviously the cooperative index $CO_{i \to j}$ is directional. Thus if nation i is the United States and j is China, then $CO_{i \to j}$ represents the cooperation of the United States with China and the equation becomes with economic development as 1 and power as 2:

$$CO_{US \to China} = -\alpha_{US,ec.dev.}(status_{US,ec.dev.} - status_{China,ec.dev.})$$
$$- \alpha_{US,power}(status_{US,power} - status_{China,power})$$

And so $d_{i-j,1}$ represents the status difference between the United States and China on the economic development dimension and $d_{i-j,2}$ represents the status difference between the United States and China on the power dimension.

Note the similarity of this equation to the joint rank definition: Joint Rank $= \alpha_1(s_{i1} + s_{j1}) + \alpha_2(s_{i2} + s_{j2})$. Differences occur in the parameters α_{i1} and α_{i2} (the parameters are actor-nation located, i being the actor-nation and j the object-nation), and in the change of signs. This change in sign (to negative) is necessary because the cooperation theorem measures two nations' joint rank by their distance and not their status sum, as in the joint rank definition. This rather subtle point is adequately explained elsewhere (Rummel, 1971: 58).

This concludes the rank and behavior section of status-field theory. Emphasis has been placed upon relating status-behavior and rank. The section began by joining, in general, some behavior dimensions to status. More specifically, there was discussion of the links between a nation's rank and its frequency of behavior, and between a nation's rank and its support of the status quo. Finally, we were led to the cooperation theorem, which develops an association between the joint ranks of two nations and their cooperative behavior.

Status Disequilibrium and Behavior

Having dealt with the behavior of nations of similar high rank, the third section of status-field theory focuses on behavior caused by status inequality.

> *Axiom 8 (Dominant Status Axiom).* Nations emphasize their dominant status and the others' subordinate status in interaction.

This provokes three corollaries.

> *Dissonance Corollary.* Status disequilibrium causes cognitive dissonance.

Any nation interacting with any other nation will emphasize its dominant status, while the other nation will emphasize its subordinate status. This dissonance between how the nation expects to be treated and how it is treated by other nations creates an imbalance.

> *Status Link Corollary.* Common statuses between nations provide them with similar interests and a communication bridge.

A plausible statement but there are anomalies. Those nations sharing a status will share a common interest and point of view concerning those not of that status. One would therefore expect to see the poor versus the rich or the strong versus the weak, but there is also contrary evidence of the strong allying with the weak—e.g., the United States with South Vietnam.

Uncertainty Corollary. The more two nations are status incongruent, the more their relationships are uncertain and the more incongruent their expectations of each other's behavior.

Axiom 9 (Economic Development Status Axiom). The more similar in economic development status, the more nations are mutually cooperative.

Nations having similar status in economic development have more to gain, economically, by cooperation than they do by conflict. Together they have the ability to exploit and become economically more developed, thus increasing their individual status.

Theoem 7. Two nations' status incongruence is correlated with their mutual status-dependent conflict behavior.

This would predict that most conflict behavior will be directed by a UT nation toward a TU nation, and least conflict behavior toward a UT nation, with TT and UU falling in between.

Theorems 8 and 9, which follow, are related; the only differences are due to the negative sign in the underdeveloped case. This is because all dimensions are relative to an international average, this average being treated as zero. All those nations below this average will have a negative value on the economic dimension; economically developed nations above the average will have positive values.

Theorem 8 (Economically Developed Conflict Theorem). For economically developed actors, status-dependent conflict behavior $CF_{i \to j} = \beta_{i1} d_{i-j,1} - \beta_{i2} d_{i-j,2}$.

Verbally, this specifies that the conflict behavior of nation i as actor nation and nation j as object nation is dependent upon their distances on both the status dimensions. Thus it is called status-dependent behavior.

Theorem 9 (Economically Underdeveloped Conflict Theorem). For economically underdeveloped actors, status-dependent conflict behavior $CF_{i \to j} = -(\beta_{i1} d_{i-j,1} - \beta_{i2} d_{i-j,2})$.

The reader might enjoy interpreting this equation in terms of US→China status differences on the economic development and power dimensions.

In this subsection of status-field threory, there have been attempts to link status disequilibrium with behavior.

Conflict/Cooperation and Status Behavior

Previously, we have seen the following two equations:

$$CO_{i \to j} = -\alpha_{i1} d_{i-j,1} - \alpha_{i2} d_{i-j,2}$$

$$CF_{i \to j} = \beta_{i1} d_{i-j,1} - \beta_{i2} d_{i-j,2}$$

The first is the cooperation theorem, and the second is the economically developed conflict theorem. Adding these, as we are allowed in linear algebra, we obtain:

$$CO_{i \to j} + CF_{i \to j} = (\beta_{i1} - \alpha_{i1}) d_{i-j,1} - (\beta_{i2} + \alpha_{i2}) d_{i-j,2}.$$

However, previous status-field theorems suggest that the parameters β_{i1}, α_{i1}, β_{i2}, α_{i2} are positive correlations—that is, between 0.0 and 1.0. Here Rummel (1971) goes on to make an assumption that I find difficult to follow. Asserting that the four parameters are close in value, he continues that $(\beta_{i1} - \alpha_{i1})$ will be near zero, while $(\beta_{i2} + \alpha_{i2})$ is near unity. He concludes that all conflict-plus-cooperation behavior must therefore be dependent upon status distances on the power dimension.

There are two steps here that need examination. The first is the assertion that all of the parameters are fairly close in value. This needs more justification. Second, if true, then it is also true that $(\beta_{i1} - \alpha_{i1})$ would reduce to zero, but it would not necessarily follow that $(\beta_{i2} + \alpha_{i2})$ approaches unity. As an illustration, suppose we assume that all the parameters are 0.25. The term $(0.25 - 0.25)$ reduces to zero, but $(0.25 + 0.25)$ becomes 0.50, which is a long way from unity. For accuracy it could be stated that conflict-and-cooperative behavior is dependent upon some weighted value of the power status distance.

Theorem 10 (Economically Developed Status Behavior Theorem). The status dependent cooperation and conflict behavior of economically developed nations to others is a function of their power incongruence, that is, $CO_{i \to j} + CF_{i \to j} = -\gamma_{i2} d_{i-j,2}$, where $CO_{i \to j}$ is nation i to j cooperative behavior, $CF_{i \to j}$ is conflict behavior, γ_{i2} is a positive parameter equalling $(\beta_{i2} + \gamma_{i2})$ and $d_{i-j,2}$ is the i–j incongruence (distance vector) of power status.

For illustration purposes, let us use the US→China dyad. The economically developed status behavior equation represents Cooperation$_{US \to China}$ + Conflict$_{US \to China}$ = $\gamma_{US,power}$ (Status difference between US and China on the power dimension). Thus, cooperation-plus-conflict between the dyads of economically developed nations is a weighted function of status difference on the power dimension.

Theorem 11 can be developed in a similar fashion, by taking the cooperation theorem and merging it with the economically underdeveloped conflict theorem. Formally this means adding the following two equations:

$$CO_{i \to j} = -\alpha_{i1} d_{i-j,1} - \alpha_{i2} d_{i-j,2}$$

$$CF_{i \to j} = -(\beta_{i1} d_{i-j,1} - \beta_{i2} d_{i-j,2})$$

Which produces:

$$CO_{i \to j} + CF_{i \to j} = -(\alpha_{i1} + \beta_{i1}) d_{i-j,1} + (\beta_{i2} - \alpha_{i2}) d_{i-j,2}.$$

Under the assumption of equality of the parameters, this is reduced to the following theorem:

Theorem 11 (Economically Underdeveloped Status Behavior Theorem).

$$CO_{i \to j} + CF_{i \to j} = -\gamma_{i1} d_{i-j,1}$$

where $\gamma_{i1} = \alpha_{i1} + \beta_{i1}$.

This would predict that status-dependent cooperation-and-conflict behavior of economically underdeveloped nations is a function of their economic development incongruence or their distance apart in rank on this status dimension.

Returning to our US→China dyad, this equation becomes:

$$\text{Cooperation}_{US \to China} + \text{Conflict}_{US \to China} =$$
$$-\gamma_{US,ec.dev.}(\text{status difference on the economic development dimension}).$$

This posits that for underdeveloped nations, the conflict-plus-cooperation behavior in a specified direction—say, from the United States to China—is a weighted difference of their relative positions on the economically developed dimension.

This ends this section on the relationship between conflict/cooperation and status incongruence.

Two Concluding Theorems

In this final section of status-field theory there is a tidying up of various loose theoretical ends. This is done via two theorems which originated in field theory.

> *Theorem 12 (Status-Time Theorem).* The status-dependent behavior of nation i to j at time t is linearly dependent on their status distance vectors at time t.

This theorem provides for simultaneous causation or influence (call it what you will) between status distances and status behavior. The simultaneity provision has been discussed fully by Rummel in "Social Time . . . " (Rummel, 1970b).

> *Theorem 13.* Behavior space is a subspace of, and therefore contained in, attribute space.

A discussion of this can be found where Axiom 7 of field theory was examined.

Status-field theory is possibly a very fruitful project step for DON. There is a wealth of hypotheses and propositions to be derived from the nine axioms and thirteen theorems that it provides.

At this time there has only been one skirmish between data and the theoretical structure. In this, Sang Woo Rhee (1972), using content-analyzed behavior data and DON-collected attribute data, tested Rummel's status-field Theorem 10. Theorem 10, though called the economically developed status behavior theorem by Rummel, is designated the "interaction theorem" by Rhee. Being an area specialist, Rhee chose China as the actor nation. The results were disappointing, providing very little support for the relationship between interaction and the power status dimension. Perhaps the data in this study—positive and negative comments in *People's Daily*—were not really suitable.

Work on status-field theory is comparatively new and, given more extensive exercise, may prove substantively rich.

THE RELATIONSHIP BETWEEN FIELD THEORY AND FACTOR ANALYSIS

I pointed out in the introductory part of this chapter that there is more than a little confusion as to the role of factor analysis in the DON Project. Let us consider the position as it is, not as it might or should be. Field theory postulates a relationship between social distance and behavior using a framework of Euclidean space. For whatever other reasons factor analysis is used (Rummel in a personal communication cited parsimony,

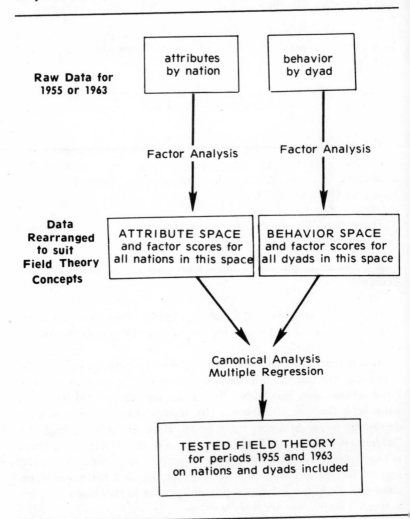

Figure 2.

uncorrelated attribute dimensions and an elegant mathematical deductive system), given that one chooses to use a linear space framework, one requires some mechanism for operationalizing the dimensions of the spaces.

Field theory requires two linear spaces: attribute and behavior. Data for these spaces can be collected on many variables, many of which are highly correlated with others. Factor analysis distills these data into the basic dimensions for the spaces. That is, factor analysis converts the raw data into data the theory requires. Thus, the spaces are empirically determined by the use of factor analysis. Factor analysis is not used in the testing of the theory; other techniques such as multiple regression and canonical analysis are used to test for the relationships between attributes and behavior. Factor analysis provides the ammunition for the testing devices. The flow diagram (Figure 2) might be illustrative. Factor analysis is the bridge between observations and the theoretical constructs of space, dimension and location.

Now one may not agree that Euclidean space is a good theoretical construct, and indeed the same model could have been tested using other techniques. One may also suspect that, since so much time had already been committed by Rummel to factor analysis and the production of these spaces, he was loath to structure the theory in any other terms than Euclidean space. All of this, however, misdirects the question. Given a theoretical framework using Euclidean space, factor analysis is an adequate operationalizing tool.

IV. THE NEEDS OF INTERNATIONAL RELATIONS IN THE EARLY 1960s AND THE ACHIEVEMENTS AND STRENGTHS OF DON

The reviewer of any extended project can easily fall into the trap of underestimating its value. By assessing the project against current needs of international relations, he may unjustly downgrade much effort. The responsible reviewer should estimate the needs of the discipline at the time the project began and, to a large extent, appraise its achievements accordingly. He should also take into account the changing needs of the profession over the period of the project and how the investigators have adapted their research to these requirements, assuming that the research is adaptable. As one of the respondents to the letter survey points out,

Standing today in 1971, it is not too difficult to see shortcomings of work done in 1965 or even in 1969. What is important . . . is the growth and lines of development that one can trace through the work. These, in my opinion, are more important than particular papers or findings.

In this section, I shall try to describe the needs of international relations as they were seen at the time of the start of DON. I shall also describe the motivations of the principal investigator and the manner in which these motivations were translated into a research plan. Finally, I shall put forward the achievements of the DON Project.

The needs of the discipline in the early 1960s have been best described—as are many other issues in international relations—by Karl Deutsch (1960). These priorities can be summarized as:

(1) a need to move away from the study of localized conflict behavior between two nations,

(2) a need to desist from studying small scale and short range conflict problems, and

(3) a need for broad surveys of data in order to know what has or is taking place in international relations.

In essence, Deutsch expressed a desire for grand international relations theory, backed by a substantial data base.

The implications of these priorities were considerable. Deutsch prescribed the collection of data on a level that had not been previously envisioned—requiring the classification and the coding of variables for all nations in the existing political system. At the time there had only been three large studies involving the collection and analysis of data: the work of Lewis Fry Richardson on arms races and deadly quarrels, Quincy Wright's study of war, and the factor analysis work of Cattell and Berry. Just beginning at this time were the data program at Yale and the Stanford studies of integration and conflict.

It was in this environment that DON was conceived. This, together with the motivations of the original three investigators, determined the course that the project took. Harold Guetzkow was involved deeply in simulation and felt that there was some need to provide empirical inputs as validation for his simulation model. Sawyer regarded the replication of the work of Cattell as being an important step forward. Whereas these two sets of motivations were no doubt instrumental in forming the original research proposal, it has been the motivations of Rummel, who has been with the project from start to finish, that have played the most important role in determining the continuing research policy. Rummel, in a personal interview with this author, has described his motivations as follows:

I saw ... that much preliminary empirical work was propositions upon which a theory could be built. Sensitive to the history of the physical sciences, I know that the breakthroughs of Galileo, Copernicus. Newton and Einstein were based upon a considerable amount of empirical work. Since such empirical work seemed to be lacking in 1961, with the exception of Lewis Fry Richardson and Quincy Wright, I felt that I myself would have to spend considerable effort in the empirical domain, in spite of my desire to be more theoretical.... My reasons were simple; empirical work needed to be done to lay the foundation for building theory, and since few people were doing it, I felt somebody had to. ... Thus if I want a theory, I had to work in the data.

Thus, all these needs and ambitions went into the conception of DON.

The overall plan for DON has been reported in "DON Project: A Five-Year Program." (Rummel, 1967a) The reader should understand that this proposal was not designed at the start of the project in 1962. On the contrary, it evolved from working with the data from 1962 until 1966 and with the motivations of Rummel described above. The work plan for that period had three phases. An outline is presented below.

Phase 1

(1) collect attribute dimensions of nations for 1955

(2) group nations according to attribute profiles

Phase 2

(1) collect behavior dimensions of nation dyads for 1955

(2) develop link between attribute and behavior spaces in social field theory

(3) determine empirical link between two spaces

(4) collect attribute dimensions of nations for 1963

(5) collect behavior dimensions of nation dyads for 1963

(6) determine the empirical link between the 1963 spaces

Phase 3

(1) collect attribute dimensions for nations, years 1950, 1960, 1965

(2) collect behavior dimensions for nation dyads, years 1950, 1960, 1965

(3) execute analysis of the Asian subsystem

(4) develop computer model of the international system based on social field theory and with parameters taken from data

These were the fundamental aims of the project. There were other more general aims concerned with the total effect of the project on the study of international relations. These were: (a) create an intellectually stimulating and critical project environment, (b) produce students who would likely contribute to a science of conflict by their own work and through their students, and (c) get results into the mainstream of academic research so that others could use them and provide critical feedback.

Much has been omitted from these plans, either by design or default, which has left weaknesses in the research design. Whether the findings of DON are considered relevant will largely depend upon the interests of the reader. That they are of considerable general importance is undeniable, that the project has succeeded in its own terms is unquestionable, that it is a personal triumph for Rummel is beyond doubt.

The findings of DON are collected in a series of research reports that have been circulated by the project. And indeed, many of these have been included in an article in *World Politics* (Rummel, 1969a). The findings are largely from the "atheoretical" period referred to in the previous chapter. Many of the results from the exploration of field theory are yet to be published, although they can be found in various research reports.

The impact of DON results on other researchers can be gauged from reference to and use of the findings. A survey of five of the leading political science journals from 1962 to 1971 was made to determine this. The survey pointed to little use of the data or the findings. In the five journals, *Journal of Conflict Resolution, Journal of Peace Research, World Politics, International Studies Quarterly* and *American Political Science Review,* there were 54 references to 29 different DON publications. Of the 54 citations, 16 referred to the techniques used, 13 to the collection of data, 20 to the empirical findings, and only 5 to the theoretical content. Without doubt, the apparent lack of DON's impact must be disappointing for Rummel. My general impression is that the work of DON has been read superficially and referenced in woolly terms.

The letter survey demonstrated that the project is appreciated more for its methodological aspects than anything else. The following brief extracts from letters show this:

> (DON) made this contribution at a time when . . . many of us talked about quantitative data and their analysis but few of us put up the goods.
>
> International relations scholars have been influenced by the DON project to apply techniques ranging from factor analysis, through discriminant function analysis . . . to canonical analysis.

The major contribution of DON has been to encourage an interest in event data.... Deutsch got us interested in attribute data but Rummel began to collect events after defining operational coding schemes.

Perhaps field theory and status-field theory, when they have been tested and the testing published, will attract more serious consideration.

But there are other components of large projects such as DON. One must take into account the students from the project. A list of those associated with the project is quite impressive and included Richard Chadwick, Raymond Tanter, Tong Whan Park, Warren Phillips, along with research associates Michael Haas, Michael Shapiro, Terry Nardin, Steven Brams, Joseph Firestone, and George Kent.

Another consideration is the experience gained from such a large project. The organizers of many current large projects have learned from the difficulties encountered in operating DON. There is no doubt in my mind that a major contribution of DON has been its pioneering attempts to formalize a large and potentially unwieldy research project. Close control was essential, and one can have nothing but admiration for the way in which it has been accomplished. The relative ease with which Rummel has been able to command large-scale financial support from various agencies underlines this.

Perhaps the major virtue of the project has been the concerted effort over a considerable period. The way in which research has progressed incrementally—with modification, adaption, and development when necessary—deserves tremendous respect. The stubbornness in sticking to this research strategy despite many adverse comments from the profession is a characteristic of DON that I find admirable.

Overall, the strengths of the project have been:

(1) clear research design, understandable by anyone who takes the trouble;

(2) methodological and technical competence;

(3) open end communication system including criticism encouraged by weekly planning sessions with all staff, a floating graduate student plan, research reports, conferences, research associateships, availability of data;

(4) strengths of research reports including
  (a) provision of method descriptions,
  (b) concern about reliability and validity,
  (c) definite commitment to communicate findings, methods, data, and theory-testing;

(5) a good student training;

(6) the utmost provision has been made for the replication of the work of DON.

Having begun this chapter by listing the requirements of international relations at the time of embarcation upon the project, we should consider the extent to which DON has satisfied these requirements. Deutsch wished for grandiose international relations theory with substantial backing from a data base. Rummel has provided a large data base available in a form suitable for exploitation by any scholar. Field theory and status-field theory are impressively grand in scale. I feel, however, that the profession views field theory as substantively barren; and that the degree to which the whole DON project will eventually be accepted and recognized may, to a large extent, depend upon the substantive contributions of status-field theory.

V. CRITICISMS OF DON

In an attempt to identify as objectively as possible the various doubts that political scientists have of the DON project, a total of 37 senior international relations academicians were surveyed by letter. The criticisms expressed in their responses to the letter survey fell into definite patterns. These major patterns of criticism cluster around nine headings—six of which attracted a large amount of attention, while three less so. The six major categories were: publication weaknesses; inductiveness of the research and triviality of findings; confusion of axioms, theorems, and propositions; theoretical consequences of DON; difficulties with explanation and causality; and policy implications of DON.

The three minor criticisms concerned the use of the New York *Times* as a data source, the use of explained variance as a research criterion, and the employment of the dyad and nation states as the entities of analysis. In the following sections, I will summarize all of these criticisms, where necessary, and comment on their validity.

PUBLICATION WEAKNESSES

It cannot be said that DON has not attempted to communicate its findings to the profession. Of the total funds employed during this whole period, something on the order of ten percent has been expended on publications of one form or another and on various panels and conferences that have taken place. There have been no less than 63 research reports from the project, which are automatically sent to an average of some 300 persons—most of whom are within the profession or allied disciplines. There has been a score of articles in various major journals.

On the other hand, good communication may be defined as "a clear, reasonably complete and consistent set of messages to a well-defined readership." The DON project did not provide "clear, reasonably complete sets of messages," nor was their readership well-defined or, in many cases, capable of understanding the message.

There are general reasons which might account for this. First, there is a real lack of journal publication space in the international relations arena. Many journals have waiting lists of two to three years. This is further aggravated by the technical aspects of projects like DON. The number of academicians capable of understanding the techniques and methodologies employed is few, while journals must cater to a more general audience. Technical articles and papers are difficult to place. If the articles are placed, their lateness adds to confusion. The lag in publication means that although a project may have changed its research concentration from, say, atheoretical data analysis to the developing and testing of a theory, for some period after the change, a wrong image is generated. Add to this the more timely communication that goes on at conferences, and the result is confusion. I am not suggesting that this is not a problem for many scholars, but it is aggravated when the work has a high technical content.

A second reason for confused communication is the magnitude of DON and the number and rapid turnover of the people associated with it. More than forty people have been associated with the project, some producing very difficult work. This expands the area covered by the project, but reduces the ability of observers to comprehend the scope of research.

A third difficulty is the general lack of interest in, and therefore awareness of, other work going on in political science. While physical scientists wait avariciously for the work of their contemporaries (for evidence of this, read Watson and Crick's account of the double helix research), political scientists are rarely so interested. The effect is to reduce the general awareness of what is going on around them.

However, these are general difficulties within the field and have more to do with the audience than the communicator. It would be unfair to leave the reader with the impression that there have not been weaknesses on the part of DON in the communication of its work.

In an attempt to surmount the difficulties in getting research published through the journals, DON has issued a series of research reports. The earliest one of these appeared in April 1966, and there have been 63 published up to July 1972. This is almost one per month—prolific indeed! Most of these have taken the format of articles, although some have been quarterly reports (a kind of project diary), while others have been research proposals. It is my opinion that the considerable expense involved in providing these reports was not fully warranted; further, these research reports have been largely responsible for the confused perception of the project.

The rate at which the research reports have been produced has resulted in a loss of control of output from the project. To some extent, the research report is the indolent channel for publication, particularly when (as is true for the DON project) the major author is also the editor. The route of publication through journals, though slow, has the saving grace of confronting reports of work with reviewers and editors. In this way, inconsistencies appearing in the work can be ironed out. But more important, it changes the attitude of the writer: if he feels that the work will be subject to careful scrutiny, then he will try to polish it appropriately. If this is not the case—as it seldom is with self-issued research reports—then there may be less effort. Indications of this can be seen in some of the research reports. Three examples follow.

(1) In Research Report 29 (Rummel, 1969b), there is much discussion of the difficulties of the model presented in Axiom 5 of the axiomatic structure of field theory. Indeed, the whole paper concerns tests of Model 1 and Model 2 as described in Axiom 5. However, on page 19 and others there is reference to Axiom 6, although the author apparently is still treating Axiom 5. Clarity regarding the axiom was essential to the whole paper.

(2) In Research Report 39 (Phillips, 1970), the author outlines a structure of 5 axioms, and then goes on to write about some mythical Axiom 6 (page 29). In the same paper, the author stresses that Equation 3 is the cornerstone of the theorem; no Equation 3 is listed.

There have also been inconsistencies across the whole collection of research reports.

(3) In Research Report 29 (Rummel, 1969b: 16), the author notes that the time axiom has come under questioning and that he is in the process of straightening this out. He subsequently achieves this in Research Report 40 (Rummel, 1970b), making the original time axiom redundant. Nevertheless, in Research Report 57 (Rhee, 1971), which presumably supersedes both 40 and 29, another DON author maintains the time axiom, without any reference or footnote acknowledging the previous doubts and final dismissal of the axiom.

These are only a few of the inconsistencies. It is my submission that these have undoubtedly influenced the image of the project.

The rapidity with which the research reports have been produced has also generated a form of deja vu in the minds of some observers of the project. This is caused by the publication in journals of what were originally research reports. The reader sees in the journal a copy of something that he read as a research report two or three years earlier. His reaction could well be, "Is this still all that they are doing?" or "Don't they ever do anything else?" or "Hasn't all of this been done before?" Many of the respondents to the letter survey mentioned this effect.

This problem is exacerbated by the similarity of a number of research reports. Many of them have an introductory section describing field theory, followed by some testing of the models. Only the very careful reader will differentiate between these reports.

All in all, more control of the publications from DON was called for. The appointment of an editor to control the output from the project would have been advantageous. Someone with an eye for the effects of the written word and the impression delivered was needed. The salary of such a person might well have been defrayed by a reduction into concentrated form of the research report series.

A second form of literary activity by DON has been the production of books. Two books have been produced, one of which has been published (Rummel, 1970c), while the other is in production and is expected in 1972 (Rummel, 1972). The first book is of high quality and will receive the attention that it undoubtedly deserves; it resulted from research during the initial two years of the project and does not include any of the substantive work from the project. The book in production (tentatively called *Dimensions of Nations*) collects all of the research reports for the period where the emphasis was the collection of attribute data—the period described in this review as "atheoretical beginnings." It is a large and well-written document and will prove as useful as the first book.

One cannot fault the idea of these books. They represent a mature effort instead of the "writing from the hip" technique which has so characterized the research reports. At the moment, a series of these books is proposed in order to bring together the work of the project. These volumes should go far to reduce the confusion within the profession, and the investigators on the project owe it to themselves to provide a clear and complete record of their decade of effort.

Finally, there must be some mention of the added difficulties in carrying out a large-scale project in Hawaii, which is over 2,000 miles from the mainland and over 4,000 miles from the cluster of acknowledged leadership in the international relations field on the east coast. The cost of travel between Hawaii and the mainland must have reduced the possibilities for meetings with other academicians—meetings at which explanation of the research effort could have been made.

In summary, it is fair to say that DON has gone out of its way to communicate findings, data, and so forth, as soon as possible. Much financial and intellectual effort has gone into this which, on reflection, does not now seem warranted. A conscious decision early in the project led to emphasis on getting research out quickly for the benefit of people in the field. In this decision, there was some tradeoff between speed of dissemination and mature reflection on the work. This point has been acknowledged by Rummel, who now feels that concentration on a regular series of books would have been more sensible.

Without doubt a most necessary task is to tidy up, in written form, the work of the ten-year project. This is a recommendation supported by many of the respondents to the letter survey. Overall, four DON books seem called for, each dealing with a particular, distinguishable segment of the research:

DON 1—(already produced; see Rummel, 1972): Descriptions of the coding, classification, and collection of the 82 nation by 236 attribute data matrix. This also contains the various nations as subsystems with the international system.

DON 2—(there are no plans for this volume): Descriptions of the coding, classification, and collection of dyadic behavior for the five data years. This would appear as a sister volume to DON 1. Both books would contain fundamental data on attribute and dyadic behavior space.

DON 3—Descriptions of the development and testing of field theory and all the variants of field theory.

DON 4—Description of status-field theory, its derivation from field theory, and how it tested.

I would strongly urge that these publications be edited by someone divorced from the project who has the technical competence to understand and evaluate the work produced. I would also suggest that the work not be published with the help of project funds. A severe test of any research work is the ease or difficulty with which it gets published.

One of the respondents commented that the research reports arrived on his desk in rapid succession, all of them looking the same and none of them providing any clue as to where the reader should start if he had the inclination to spend, say, a day learning about field theory. To this end, it would seem sensible to produce a research report which would index the various research reports to aid the reader interested in a particular component of project work.[1]

A similar list could be developed for all the various components of DON research and would prove immensely valuable to the research report audience.

THE INDUCTIVE NATURE OF
DON AND TRIVIALITY OF FINDINGS

The most frequent criticism made about DON has been the triviality of its findings. This is due to the project's original emphasis on inductive processes and a reliance upon factor analysis which has constantly been seen as far too methodologically rigorous and technical for the study of international relations.

In an attempt to provide the reader with an overview of these criticisms, I have collected the reports of various reviewers of DON articles submitted to journals for possible publication. The assessment of articles sent to journals is normally anonymous; and in this section I shall respect this tradition. I have included in this survey four articles which were produced from the early atheoretical period. All of the articles have been or are being published in journals or books.

"Dimensions of Conflict Within and Between Nations" by Rummel: Twenty-two behavior variables, some of them concerned with foreign conflict and others with domestic conflict, were factor-analyzed. The analysis generated various factors which were used with regression techniques to demonstrate that domestic and foreign conflict were empirically separate. A reader for the *Journal of Conflict Resolution* made the following observations:

> I feel that you have permitted some exciting substantive research to get submerged in a welter of methodological preoccupations. I would have preferred that you completely reverse your methodological emphasis, putting much more on your data gathering and coding operations and less on your manipulations of the data . . . your reader could benefit from a heavier dose of interpretation and discussion of your findings, with less on the statistical analysis of them.

> I sorely missed a heavier concentration on theoretical formulation: why you selected the variables and dimensions you did; some hypotheses and justifications; where and how your inquiry fits into the larger framework of past and present research.

"Some Dimensions in the Foreign Behavior of Nations" by Rummel: This article was, to some extent, a continuation of the previous one. The number of variables was increased to 94 (as against 22 in the previous study) and the number of nations included was 82. The summarized results of the study were:

(1) Many activities of nations are highly correlated with each other and can be structured meaningfully in terms of several independent dimensions.

(2) Many diverse international activities of nations form independent patterns of relationships that can be identified as participation, conflict, aid, ideology, popularity, South American, and ideology dimensions;

(3) Basic indicators that index some of the independent clusters of relationships among the many diverse activities of nations are trade, threats, technical assistance and relief fellowships received, net percent of UN votes for the United States, ratio of visitors to population, air distance from the United States, and ratio of immigrants to population.

(4) The magnitude of participation by a nation in the international system is a result of its economic development and power capability. Its conflict behavior is a phenomenon dependent on its relation to other nations.

The following comments were made by readers of the *American Political Science Review*, who finally rejected the article:

What about the substantive side? Personally, I learned nothing from the factor analysis that I did not understand pretty well before. The major conclusion—that international behavior was somehow patterned—is hardly more than a platitude as long as the nature of this pattern is not contrasted with other possible or historical patterns. The description of the clusters is hardly new nor is their discovery on the basis of factor analysis surprising, as the author admits.

Amusingly, another reader of this paper was surprised that the analysis showed that conflict and cooperation were on different continuums. He felt that since this was so counter-intuitive, it must be the result of faulty methods.

"Dimensions of Dyadic War, 1830-1952" by Rummel: This analysis was of 211 violent conflicts from the period 1820-1952. The following empirical propositions were drawn from the analysis:

(1) The intensity of violence is the most central dimension along which to compare the variation in violence between groups, whether nations or otherwise.

(2) Cultural and racial distance between groups is largely unrelated to the intensity of their violent conflict.

(3) For violence between groups in general, time (date of war) has a slight positive relationship to the intensity of violence. For violence between nations, however, time is inversely related to months of involvement—indicating that there is a trend for the duration of violence between nations to become shorter.

Readers for the APSR made the following remarks:

This report itself . . . produces a curiously unimpressive set of conclusions. Thus the mathematically unsophisticated but otherwise knowledgeable international relations specialist might say, "If that is all the technique can produce, it's not worth the bother."

Finally, the author's six propositions strike the reader as trite, imprecise, and even ambiguous—an odd result of mathematical analysis.

Because we have data and new methods of processing data, this does not relieve us of the necessity to ask interesting questions and develop non-trivial hypotheses . . . the author has failed to do either.

"The Patterns of Dyadic Foreign Conflict for 1963" by Hall and Rummel: Five patterns of dyadic foreign behavior were delineated for 1963. These were: negative communications, violence intensity, warning acts, defensive acts, and negative sanctions. The purpose of the paper was to compare the amount of variance accounted for by these patterns with that accounted for in the 1955 data set. This allowed some gauging of the data stability.

This paper was rejected by both the APSR and *International Studies Quarterly* before being accepted by *Multivariate Behavioral Research.* A reader for the APSR made the following comment:

[The article] is merely a set of numbers straight out of a computer. We are given all sorts of methodological tidbits, including almost needless rotations and results of different analyses. But almost no effort is devoted to interpreting the findings in any theoretical sense, or even explicating their substance.

And from a reader for ISQ, perhaps the most vituperative attack:

I have the uncanny sense that the author has not the slightest interest in understanding (let alone communicating) anything about

international relations. His only concern seems to be with perform-
ing elegant mathematical operations on ill-defined constructs bearing
weird abbreviated names. . . . What is more irritating is the steadfast
refusal of the author to provide any interpretation of his results.
Nowhere does he discuss the implications of his work for the
understanding of international conflict. After a complex excursion
into matrix algebra, one would hope to find some payoff, some
better understanding of dyadic conflict behavior. Instead each
excursion ends abruptly with yet another data table filled with
abstract numbers. Apparently, these numbers represent little more
to the author than a new base on which to mount still another
excursion.

In summary, DON has been subjected to much criticism concerning the
triviality or inductive nature of its work; I would agree with the latter but
not the former. These particular criticisms of DON now seem to have
subsided mainly because of the change in the substance of the research.
Even so, it seems that some of the early criticism was badly specified and
should have confronted the implied theoretical assumptions behind the
development of the paradigm. Assumptions such as linearity or additivity,
for example, are fundamental and deserve careful attention. It would also
have been interesting to suggest other than linear procedures and compare
the findings from these.

CONFUSION OF AXIOMS, THEOREMS, AND PROPOSITIONS

Many discussions in political science go adrift because of definitional
differences—the participants use the same words while thinking of entirely
incompatible concepts. This confusion may be accentuated by varying
definitions of axioms, theorems, and propositions, which indeed have
clouded some aspects of DON research. The confusion, however, has not
been entirely semantic. Certain concepts have undergone changes in
definitional status during the course of the research. I include below the
definitions which I use in this discussion:

> Axiom—an initial proposition in a mathematical system not proved in
> that system and assumed "true." Sets of axioms are characterized
> by: (1) consistency—i.e., neither they nor any theory deducible from
> them are contradictory; (2) comprehensiveness, i.e., they adequately
> encapsule the particular construct of reality; and (3) there is no
> redundancy, i.e., the axioms are not deducible from one another.
>
> Theorem—a deduced proposition in a mathematical system, as "true" as
> the axiom.

Proposition—any statement but normally an empirical statement, unless otherwise indicated.

Confusion and some suspicion have resulted from the various changes between these terms as the DON project has progressed and attempted to eliminate logical inconsistency. One of the original constructs has proceeded through all three of these categories: "B-space is a subset of A-space" began as a theoretical proposition, continued as an axiom, and has finally been classified in status-field theory as a theorem.

Initially, all of the original constructs of field theory were classified as theoretical statements (Rummel, 1965a: 185). But as Rummel points out in a footnote (1969b: 10), "They functioned as axioms in the theoretical development and I thought of them as such." Eventually all of the original theoretical propositions were promoted to axioms.

As we have seen, field theory is based upon seven axioms. Rummel further divides these into the initial four, which he considers to be "analytical," and the final three, which he classifies as "empirical." In a private communication, he has asserted that the first four axioms supply the ground rules for the final three. These three depend not only on their internal empirical refutability, but also on the relevancy of the first four to international relations. I will discuss this division further in Chapter VI.

Much of the work of the years 1965 to 1971 has attempted to streamline this axiomatic structure. A recent research report (Rummel, 1971: 6) relates that the original seven can be reduced to three:

These three (which are said to describe Field Theory) are reduced from the original seven axioms of Field Theory. Since their initial publication, empirical and theoretical work has shown an interdependence (redundancy) among the axioms which, along with some changes in wording, permitted the reduction of the number to the three given here.

Of the original first four axioms, two appear to have been eliminated. Originally, Axiom 4 stated that "nations are located as vectors in attribute space and coupled into dyads in behavior space." Rearranging the wording in status-field theory has made the original Axiom 4 redundant. The same cannot be said about the original Axiom 3, which stated that "attribute and behavioral spaces are generated by a finite set of linear independent dimensions." The aim of this axiom in field theory was to make the whole of the axiomatic structure operational and, therefore, susceptible to testing. In status-field theory, however, it is a theorem deduced from one of the axioms.

Moving on to the empirical axioms of field theory (5, 6, and 7), 6 has been completely eliminated by the arguments appearing in the "Social Time and International Relations" paper (Rummel, 1970b). The necessary word changes in status-field theory accommodate the original intention of the axiom. Axiom 7 has had a curious history. It began as a theoretical proposition in the original formulation of the structure, was then promoted to an axiom and finally relegated to a theorem in status-field theory. This axiom and Axiom 5 of field theory have always been linked. Axiom 5 posits that the distance vectors in A-space that connect nations are the social forces determining the location of dyads in B-space. This is construed as meaning that B-space is dependent on A-space. Mathematically, this implies that B-space is a subspace of A-space, making the original Axiom 7 of field theory redundant as an axiom.

Many of the comments on the axiomatic structure appear, however, to somehow miss the mark. Does it really matter whether some statement is called an axiom or proposition until it has been decided or agreed that the paradigm within which it has been placed is a relevant one or at least a substantively fruitful one? Are not the more fundamental questions concerned with the intuitive appeal of Euclidean space? Should there not be more concern with the implied assumptions of linear space as against nonlinear space? Is Rummel's interpretation of what Lewin or Wright meant by "field" consonant with other views of its meaning? The discussion of whether this or that is an axiom or not assumes a basic paradigm correctness. It's rather like discussing whether hanging or gassing is the better form of execution before discussing the advisability of capital punishment. Discussion at the axiom level clouds the issue and diverts attention from the paradigmatic issue.

IS FIELD THEORY A THEORY?

The models that have been derived from Axiom 5 of field theory have attracted much attention from the critics. The reader will remember that there have been two models derived from Axiom 5. They were labelled MOdels 1 and 2 and have been discussed previously. The most common doubt concerns the theoretical consequence of these models. One of the critics doubts that the model has any.

> What it (DON) has generated in the way of so-called "theory" is sophisticated description based on a conceptually limited—even *ad hoc*—data base.

> My view is that the author's basic schemes should not be called a theory in any social scientific sense. If by theory, we mean a

formation which—*inter alia*—describes, and then accounts for observed regularities of a fairly specific nature, we have something less than a theory here. I'd call it a taxonomy, and I'd call his axioms empirical definitions and epistomological propositions; there seems to be nothing explanatory or predictive in them except in the trivial sense of the word. My first criticism, then, is that we have something less than a theory. Secondly, and this may be equally idiosyncratic, I find it difficult to take seriously a set of results based on single, cross-sectional set of observations from one point in time.

To this particular critic, Rummel has replied in a letter as follows:

Earlier generations (here again, I'm speaking of generations separated by a few years) conceived of theory as a persuasively articulated set of verbal notions suggesting hypotheses to be tested in some manner. Subsequent generations have refined theory to mean a logically interconnected set of propositions with operationalizable (a clumsy word unfortunately having religious meaning for many behavioralists) terms and a specification of independent and dependent variables. The most recent generation (of which I count myself a member because of an unusual background in philosophy, physics, and mathematics—but unfortunately, not in English) of IR scholars have come to understand by theory an analytic system, only partially given content and from which predictions about phenomena can be deduced. The test of whether such a theory is indeed a theory is whether it can be empirically falsified (a test my field theory meets), and the test of whether predictions about IR can be derived from the theory is the degree to which the predictions accord with observations.

I have some sympathy for both of the positions delineated here and indeed am perhaps being just a little unfair to the original critic since his remarks resulted from a review of a particular DON study (Rummel, 1969b). In that report, the two models derived from Axiom 5 of field theory were confronted with the 1955 data and some random data.

Let us leave Model 1 aside, as it did poorly and was eventually dropped. Model 2 takes the form:

$$w_{i \to j,k} = \sum_{\ell=1}^{p} \alpha_{i,\ell} \, d_{i \to j,\ell}$$

Using canonical correlation and the 1955 data, estimates were obtained for the parameters $\alpha_{i,\ell}$. Canonical correlation computes these parameters while maximizing the correlation (least squares) between both sides of an equation. Rummel argues in a private communication that he is interested solely in the fit of the model to the data, as against an interest in the value of parameters which would in reality only provide a description of the data. The argument is concerned with intentions. Rummel's position is that his main interest is in determining how well the model derived from the axiomatic structure stands up to the data in terms of the accountable variance. The critics feel that all that has been provided is a description of the data for a particular time period.

At the same time, while establishing the goodness of fit of the model, Rummel has determined parameters for the model; and while he only achieves this for the one time period, then he may be perceived as having only described the data for that year. But if on analysis of the other years (1950, 1960, 1963, and 1965), there is some constancy found in the value of the parameters $\alpha_{i,\varrho}$ then he will have something that is law-like. If, for example, the parameter $\alpha_{China,power}$ (i.e., the parameter that operates with China as the actor and along the attribute dimension power) is found to be constant over different object-nations of the dyads, and across the various years that are chosen for the collection of data, then this is more than a mere description of the data; it will be a law. In the same way that while on earth—whatever the size of the ball, angle of the leaning tower, and height that the ball is dropped from—the parameter in the law of a falling body remains fairly constant. It is true that this value changes if the ball is let fall, say, on the moon; but it will still remain constant wherever this is done on the moon. Moving from the earth to the moon in determining the parameter incorporated in the law of falling bodies can be compared with moving from actor-nation to actor-nation along the same attribute dimensions in field theory.

Summarizing this, Rummel states that his intention has been to test the efficacy of the model he derived from field theory by fitting it to data. His critics feel that all he has done is to provide a description of the data collected for the one year. Since the model is refutable, Rummel argues, it is a theory of sorts; exactly how good a theory will be measured by the constancy of the parameter. If, after testing for all of the years 1950, 1955, 1960, 1963, and 1965, there is some constancy in the parameters $\alpha_{i,\varrho}$, this will indicate a law of international relations. This testing, as yet, is incomplete.

DIFFICULTIES WITH PREDICTION, EXPLANATION AND CAUSE

There has been some criticism concerning the notions of prediction, explanation, and cause expressed by the DON work in general and

Rummel in particular. The specific passage that attracted much of this critical attention appeared in Rummel (1967b: 453).

> The term *explanation* adds nothing to the word *cause*. Although laden in the social sciences with a surplus meaning associated with *verstehen*, a feeling of understanding, of getting the sense of something, the explanation of phenomena is nothing more than *being able to predict or mathematically relate* phenomena. To explain an event is to be able to predict it. To explain that the Roman Empire fell because of disunity and moral decay is to say that, given the presence of these two elements in an empire with the characteristics of the Roman Empire, the empire will break up and be conquered.
>
> Prediction itself is based on the identification of causal relations, i.e., regularity.

This particular section drew the attention of two critics who commented:

> The causation argument probably claims too much; certainly as offered it is imprudent.
>
> I must register a strong personal dissent from your use of "cause" and "explain." It ignores the fact that one can get sufficiently strong correlations to permit consistent predictions, without telling us much about "How come?" In my book, explanation's adequacy is peculiar to the state of the art at a given moment, and (even worse) the level of knowledge of the audience or reader. The discovery of a statistical regularity may be *necessary* to identifying *cause,* but far from *sufficient.* Would you agree with the curve-fitters who claim they have an "explanation" when all they have is a good fit to their data?

Rummel's reaction to this appeared in a private communication to the critic:

> As for your position on causation and explanation—well I guess this is a very deep difference between us in methodology. I do agree with the curve fitters. I think that a curve that fits the data points is an explanation of those data points. One of many explanations, of course. Which fit to the points you decide to accept depends on which of these curves has a better fit again to existing theories or the theory you are trying to build. All the great advances in science have come through curve fitting. I think this was true with Galileo, with Kepler, and with Newton. At first, the curves that they fitted, the variables they employed, and the nature of the function was strange. But with familiarity over time comes the feeling that these things belong together and with this feeling come notions of there being a causative relationship. After one is used to dealing with the curve

that is fitted, that is, a function for a particular curve, one then begins to impute causative ideas to the variables involved.

Rummel's position as expressed at that time was that prediction is equivalent to explanation. If you could predict then you could explain, or symmetrically, if explanation was accomplished, then so was prediction. This is a position held by Hempel (1965).

This is no longer Rummel's position, although for some time there may be some work which fails to reflect this change, due to publication delays. His present position is that explanation and prediction are symmetrical, but only at the logical level. At the operational level—that is, in the world of scientific endeavor—there is an asymmetry; while an explanation assumes an ability to predict, prediction does not equivalently assume an ability to explain. Consequently, Rummel's position can best be summed up in a statement that explanation is a higher form of scientific endeavor than prediction; whereas predictions are true or false, explanations are acceptable or not. And although part of this acceptability may depend on the accuracy of derived predictions, other components such as intuition are involved in the acceptability of an explanation. This position is similar to that adopted by Hanson (1958).

Recently, there has been much emphasis on a causal approach to the study of international relations. It is argued that our efforts should be directed toward practical aspects of controlling international relations, as against an academic exercise involving understanding only. There has indeed been a trend in this direction—a search for the causes and effects of international behavior, the "knobs and levers" of international interaction.

Two types of analysis of relationships between variables can be identified: scalar and vector. (The reader should not get confused here with the definition of scalar and vector used in linear algebra.) A scalar statement is concerned only with the *magnitude* of the relationship between variables. The vector statement is concerned with both the magnitude and *direction* of this relationship. An example of the former would be some form of correlation coefficient between a series of variables; the latter would be characterized by some regression equation type of analysis. My preference is for the vector as against the scalar statement. Although the researcher can never "prove" the directional component of the vector statement, he at least makes some effort to consider the direction of dependence. He has chosen a dependent variable and a set of independent variables. A vector analysis of relationships forces this a priori thinking (see Hilton, 1972).

Field theory apparently fits in completely with this preference for prescribing the direction of dependence between variables. Verbally, it states that "social distance provides the force for international behavior," or more simply, the behavior of one nation toward another is dependent upon their vector distances apart on various attributes. Mathematically, this is expressed as:

$$w_{i \rightarrow j,k} = \sum_{\ell=1}^{p} \alpha_{i,\ell} d_{i \rightarrow j,\ell}$$

This is a vector statement of the relationship between behavior of a dyad ($w_{i \rightarrow j}$) and attribute distances ($d_{i \rightarrow j}$). It states mathematically that behavior is dependent upon attribute distance. Canonical analysis determines the magnitude of the relationship; a priori theorizing prescribes the direction of influence.

But after all this, do we have a causal explanation? I think not. Phrasing axioms and theorems in causal terms and formalizing this using dependent and independent variables does not go all the way to specifying a causal relationship. It comes down to some final belief of a causal link between attribute distance and behavior based upon content-full theory. And while field theory may be able to predict behavior from attribute distance, it is relatively content-free.

I know of no social science where explanation is attempted without a structural set of simultaneous equations with time lags included. Field theory and status-field theory do not have this characteristic and, although it is not strictly necessary to have multi-equation systems with lagged variables, the fact that field theory is without these adds to my doubts.

But Rummel's position is not a lesser position; it is a different position, one which many statisticians uphold. Predictive statistics are valid, and any consequent parameter stability will much facilitate the kind of forecasting that Rummel has envisioned.

POLICY IMPLICATIONS OF DON

DON's claims concerning the political applications of research are contained in Research Report 36 (Phillips and Rummel, 1969). Briefly, these claims included an ability to define causal inputs to behavior, control variables, causal consequences. The results would also, it was claimed, "inform planners about nation capabilities and intents, behavioral regularities, causal influences." There would be identification of "immediate and long run causes of hostility, tension, crisis, conflict, aggression and war between nations." Work on DON, it was further claimed, "ties this knowledge to a set of system oriented models by which long range projections and forecasts eventually may be made." As well as this, the data would enable the construction of computer simulations which would "help give the future context—a future state of the system—that will serve as initial and limiting conditions to inform policy judgments."

DON evidently sees its role as one of using social science to provide accurate background forecasts about the international environment which will help in the planning of long-range foreign policy postures.

The development of a data bank has almost been achieved. At the end of the project period, data will have been collected on over 200 attribute and behavior variables for the five time periods, 1950, 1955, 1960, 1963, and 1965. The computer model can also be realized once the various parameters are estimated and are shown to be empirically stable over time. It will not only allow some experimentation with a model of the international system, it will also enable a gauging of the speed of response of the system to various inputs. This will aid the forward planners, determining for them the kinds of lead time desirable in planning. The computer model is in the process of development.

However, there are substantive claims of an ability "to identify the primary factors and causal elements bearing upon nation behavior and conflict" which, in my estimation, are not easily realizable. Many of these claims stem from the efficacy of the field theory model:

$$w_{i \to j,k} = \sum_{\ell=1}^{p} \alpha_{i,\ell} d_{i \to j,\ell}$$

First, let us look at the left-hand side of the equation—the dependent variable (behavior). To all intents and purposes, dependent variables are the "effects" or phenomena that one is interested in influencing, changing, or predicting. On the right-hand side of the equation, we have the independent variables—attribute distances. These are the variables which determine the dependent variable. If these are to be of direct and practical use in controlling phenomena such as conflict, they must be manipulable. This is a vulnerability of the DON model. We have seen that the dimensions which act as independent variables in the model are produced by the factor analysis technique. This technique usually produces dimensions that are intangible, that are distillations of other variables. To this extent they are not controllable. A decision maker cannot affect any particular behavior with "controls" that are intangible.

The testing of field theory thus far illustrates this, although this does not presume that there will be no remedial action taken in the future. Of the fifteen dimensions of attribute space delineated in the 1955 data (dimensions have proved constant over time, so these comments apply to other years), three are categorized as primary dimensions: economic development, political orientation, and size (Rummel, 1972). These three dimensions alone account for 40.1% of the total variance in attributes. All are intangible dimensions. One is forced to choose an indicator for these dimensions. The indicator must load heavily upon the dimension. Those chosen by DON for each of these dimensions (and remember these are the most predictive and, therefore, the most powerful in causing changes in the dependent variable) are: energy consumption per capita, freedom of group opposition (which, incidentally, is measured trichotomously), and population size (Rummel, 1972). None of these indicators is inherently manipulable. And indeed, if you include the first eight dimensions (which have a combined total of almost 60% of the explained variance in the attribute data), only one of these has an indicator which is manipulable. This is foreign conflict behavior which has "number of threats" as an indicator. However, foreign conflict behavior only accounts for 4.6% of the total variance and is, therefore, less powerful in a controlling sense. A list of the first eight dimensions, their proportion of the variance and their allocated indicators is presented below:

(1) Economic development	20.0	energy consumption per capita	
(2) Political orientation	9.0	freedom of group opposition	
(3) Size	11.1	population	
(4) Catholic culture	3.6	Roman Catholic population/ total population	
(5) Foreign conflict behavior	4.6	number of threats	
(6) Density	4.3	population/national land area	
(7) Oriental culture	3.2	religious groups	
(8) Domestic conflict behavior	3.4	domestic deaths	

I feel that the model will allow little control of international behavior. The alleged causes of behavior, the attributes, are not readily changed. And while the model may eventually allow prediction of nation behavior, much in the way that the laws of motion predict the movement of planets, the ability to control behavior is not really possible. This adds to my previously expressed doubts about the causality of field theory. While predictions of international behavior do not require a causal relationship, control over such behavior would.

Thus I feel that some of Rummel's claims concerning the political usefulness of field theory are overstated. It would appear that field theory can only provide some forecast of the behavior trends of nations. When the computer simulation model is developed, providing stable coefficients are found, then some experimentation with a model of the international system may well be possible.

Nevertheless, field theory and status-field theory may score in a more indirect fashion. If a decision maker can be persuaded that status differences account for behavior, it will certainly restructure his manner of operating. Operating theories based upon balance of power and deterrence may be swept aside to make way for a new mode of analyzing political problems. Thus there may be some indirect shaping of the manner in which decision makers view the world.

MINOR CRITICISMS

Many of the respondents in the letter survey pointed out minor irritations about the project. There are three of these: one concerned with the data, the second concerned the use of the dyad as an entity, and the third concerned the use of the "amount of variance explained" as the criterion for successful testing.

The data. Some of the respondents have expressed doubt concerning the use of the New York *Times.* A sample appears below:

> Use of the New York *Times,* as you are aware, understates actual conflict since much more occurs than is reported in the American press. This becomes a bigger problem when you measure negative dyadic communication in other countries. How about sampling various national presses? E.g., with respect to CPR [Chinese Peoples Republic], *NCNA Bulletin* is readily available as well as *Peking Review.*

McCormick (1969) has produced an answer to these and other similar comments which would meet most of the questions. He argues that although the American press does provide an inaccurate source of absolute conflict data, it does not mean that it is an inaccurate source of the patterns of behavior. Since DON is concerned with patterns of behavior only, the loss of accuracy would seem minimal.

I feel that this form of criticism is relatively trivial and not nearly as important as others that can be made concerning the data. For instance, since behavior data are of varying quality compared to the attribute data, one might ask what effect these heterogeneous or unbalanced data would have on the testing of the model. After all, the field theory model is deterministic with supposedly no error term.

Furthermore, the data from the New York *Times* are by definition event data. There are dangers in developing theories, particularly in conflict analysis, where variables are defined as a form of behavior. If, for instance, violence is defined exclusively as a form of behavior, then when this behavior is present there is violence; when it is not present, there is no violence. This might imply a value bias. For example, a recent killing of eleven Israeli athletes by Arabs would no doubt be coded as an act of terrorism. But where will the nonbehavioral violence of producing Palestinian refugees be coded? Will it even surface in an analysis as violence? These are more important questions. And ones that most behavioralists must confront but rarely do.

The use of the dyad as the behavioral entity and the nation as attribute entity. There has been some concern over the use of the dyad as against, say, the triad. The question asked is: Does this eliminate some of the more subtle relationships and behavior between nations? This has been combatted in two ways in a private communication from Rummel: theoretically, any triad can be analyzed by mathematically breaking the triad into a dyad; second, testing may eventually show that the analysis of the triads adds nothing to the amount of variance explained. However, as yet none of this has been tested and despite these arguments and stated intentions, I still retain an intuitive unease that something may be lost. A respondent to the letter survey who shares this unease commented:

Will Rummel ever pay much attention to multiadic linkage possibilities, like the effects of alliances on whole clusters of relational data? . . . the Nye-Keohane special issue of *International Organizations* on Transnational Politics fundamentally disagrees with a between-two-nation focus.

There has also been some criticism for taking the nation-state as the level of analysis. The following is an example:

The major criticism at the theoretical level of the DON Project is its concentration on nations. In this respect, multivariate complex models have advanced beyond analysis since they include nations, sub-national groups, multinational corporations, INGO's, BINGO's and the various interactions between all these groups.

Rummel argues, in a private communication, that although one would ideally like to bring into reckoning many of the varying levels that the respondent prescribes (is this not what a general theory should do?), this would provide other serious research complications. For example, while nations have a GNP, INGOs have nothing that is comparable. While nations have embassies, guerrilla groups do not. It is a matter of choosing the level of analysis that enables consistency in comparison and the consequent ease in defining data requirements. However, one wonders whether it is sensible to let data availability dictate one's theory.

The "Amount of Variance Explained" Criterion. The criterion used by most researchers in quantitative international relations is the amount of variance that a model accounts for. This is also true of DON, where the dangers are considerable if this criterion alone is used. Throughout the DON reports, there is an emphasis on maximizing the variance explained, since this describes goodness of fit of theory to data. An example of this has been produced in a private communication from Rummel: "My feeling is that Field Theory will continue to test out as it has, but will not be able to reduce the amount of unpredicted variance of behavior to something below 25 percent."

The danger in this emphasis occurs after some series of testing, when there may be a need to decide which particular research path to follow. On a large project where costs are high, the investigators must make decisions which are often irreversible. The only objective criterion appears to be the predictability of the models which, in some cases, may lead to the adoption of the wrong research route. Such dangers are not entirely hypothetical on large-scale projects such as DON.

In reality, however, other criteria are used. One would take account not only of the ability to confront data, but also reason and intuition. The researcher would take into account the common sense behind the choice of the model, and also any feeling that he might have concerning the "rightness" of a particular model. However, on transmitting one's preferences to other academicians, one is reluctant to say feebly, "Well, I liked this model better; it seemed to make more sense to me; I somehow felt this model was the right one." The transmission of preferences for individual models is normally accompanied by some term denoting the amount of variance explained.

There are other more esoteric dangers. This pressure to account for the variance of data sets leads to an approach emphasizing predictive against explanatory power. This can be disadvantageous, as cancer research has shown. The emphasis on prediction of cancer has produced much study on the correlates such as smoking or cyclamates which may help to reduce its incidence; but we still have little understanding of how cancer starts, how it continues, and how it eventually kills. This has resulted from the need for instant relevance in cancer research which, until now, the study of international relations has managed to avoid. Nevertheless, it does point to the dangers of relying upon predictability only as criterion for determining research thrust.

VI. REFLECTIONS ON THE DEVELOPMENT OF DON

There is much evidence suggesting that DON has not had the impact on the profession that one would have thought so large an IR project should have. Referencing of DON has been badly done, and some ferociously critical treatment of the work has occurred. This criticism, to which the project has been sensitive, has undeniably led to various changes in the research thrust when appropriate. As a result, over the ten-year period, DON has gone through the different phases and changes that I discussed earlier. In this chapter I will try to place the criticism and subsequent changes within a history of science context. I will employ the Lakatos "sophisticated falsificationist" model to this end (Lakatos and Musgrave, 1970).

Lakatos holds that the "bold conjectures and austere refutations" position of Popper, although more logical and pragmatic than that of the savage naif falsificationist, does not consider the development of theory in terms of a research program. In an attempt to get around this weakness, Lakatos proposes the "sophisticated falsificationist." He allows that a theory is scientific if it has corroborated evidence or content over its predecessor. Thus, if a theory has new empirical content and part of that content is verified, it can be considered acceptable as a scientific theory. This is in contrast to the naif falsificationist who holds that only a theory that can be falsified will be accepted as scientific. Consequently, a sophisticated falsificationist regards a theory as falsified if and only if another theory has been proposed and (1) the second theory has increased empirical content over the first—that is, it produced new facts not probable or even forbidden by the first; (2) the second theory explains the success of the first; and (3) some of the excess content of the second theory is corroborated.

In this manner, theories are not considered with facts in isolation, but also with the other theories available at that time. Thus, one deals with series of theories rather than a single theory. As Lakatos continues, "no experiment, experimental report, observation statement or well corroborated low level hypothesis alone can lead to falsification. There is no falsification before the emergence of a better theory" (Lakatos and Musgrave, 1970: 119).

Success for a theory development occurs in this framework when there is a progressive problem shift—that is, the new theory or modification includes the previous theory and adds more empirical content to it. Failure occurs when there is a degenerative problem shift such that the newer version of the theory does not lead to an increase in empirical content.

Although there may be refutations of parts of the theory, this in itself should not produce the abandonment of the theory. A theory would be discarded only when it had moved into a degenerative problem shift or there emerged a better theory. In terms of DON, it is important to remember this.

A research program thus consists of two parts. The first is a hard inner core of the program. The second is a series of auxiliary hypotheses which form a protective belt around the hard core. While these may be discarded as a result of testing, the hard core remains. This core is "irrefutable" by the decision of the researchers, and any factual anomalies result in changes in the protective belt of auxiliary hypotheses, not the dismissal of the hard core.

We see, therefore, that this framework or model of research development puts forward the existence of co-present heuristics. The first, the negative heuristic, denies any vulnerability of the inner core of the program. The positive heuristic provides a path of hypothesis stepping stones which allow a problem shift and thus the survival of the program. Each incremental step in research must add to the empirical content. Should this occur, refutations or anomalies will not topple the research program and are really disregarded. Lakatos feels that if this model for the development of a research program is followed, there is a rational growth of knowledge, unspoiled by savage and possibly premature rejection by falsification alone.

Let us leave Lakatos for the moment and return to DON. Any examination of the impact of DON upon international relations raises numerous questions. Why has DON had so little impact? Why are references to DON so few and so vague? Why has so large a project produced so few doctorates? And why have these Ph.D.s been entirely within the linear space paradigm favored by Rummel? Why—despite relatively poor results from the testing of field theory (relative in the sense that field theory is deterministic not probabilistic, and so explained variance should be that much higher)—has the theory not been rejected?

Do the results from continued testing of Model 2 and status-field theory warrant continuing the paradigm? If so, how will the paradigm ever be put to the crucial test? What would be a crucial test of field theory and status-field theory?

There are many more questions that one could add to these, and indeed some may have been answered in previous parts of the review. But the most intriguing question of all is why has DON provoked such strong hostility from international relations scholars in general. A heuristic use of the Lakatos model may allow us a glimpse at possible reasons.

As we saw, Lakatos suggests various characteristics of the sophisticated falsificationist procedure. The first is the generation of the inner core which is pronounced irrefutable—in some way beyond question, and there is no testing of this inner core. DON would appear to have two components within its inner core, one derived from the original atheoretical period and the other derived from the field theory era. The first is the methodological statement concerning Euclidean space which has its basis in factor analysis. The second is the basic theoretical statement that "social distance causes behavior." Neither of these core concepts has ever been confronted by the data; they are inviolate. And although DON did progress theoretically, the theory still had its basis in linear space and the causation of behavior by social distance.

Less inviolate, however, has been the middle-range protective belt of auxiliary hypotheses that have surrounded the inner core. A list of these would include both of the field theory models that have been tested and status-field theory, which has only been partially tested.

Thus the problem shift from Model 1 to Model 2 to status-field theory can be described as progressive, in Lakatos' terms, if there has been an increase in empirical content in moving from one middle-range hypothesis to a subsequent one. A second condition is that some of this excess content be corroborated. And inspection leads one to the conclusion that Model 2 does have excess empirical content over Model 1 and, since it also tests better, part of this excess content would appear to be corroborated. A similar inspection of the second problem shift from Model 2 to status-field theory also indicates an increase in empirical content; as yet this has not been corroborated.

We see, therefore, that Rummel, in terms of his research program, has behaved as a sophisticated falsificationist. And, if this policy were continued, he would presumably discard the theory only when the research program went into a degenerative problem shift, and another theory was proposed which allowed a progressive problem shift within another program.

The reason that Rummel and field theory have received such unfriendly reactions from international relations scholars lies in the "irrefutable" inner core. While little attention has been given to the theoretical portion of this core, except to doubt the substantive content, much antagonism has been directed toward the methodological component: linear space with its basis in factor analysis. The belief that social phenomena can be mapped into linear space finds very few takers. This and its technical appliance, factor analysis, have been at the center of researchers' doubts concerning DON's research.

While operating as a sophisticated falsificationist, Rummel has argued as a naif falsificationist. And it is my belief that this alone has produced much of the dissatisfaction with field theory. In a Kuhnian sense, it has lead to nonacceptance of the theory, despite the students from the project that have been taken into other schools. Indeed there is evidence that some of the DON students have changed their paradigm perspective. One wonders whether this can be linked to the rejection of field theory. Rummel has aggravated this problem somewhat. As one reviewer commented: "Who else but a paradigmatic true believer would write a clear, cogent 500 page text on applied factor analysis. . . . But from the point of view of paradigm implementation and elaboration, an applied book makes sense."

The depth to which Rummel holds the importance of the methodological paradigm is also demonstrated by his training of the students from the project. Rummel wrote that one of the concerns of DON was to "produce students who would later contribute to a science of conflict by their own work and through their students. *This meant getting students enmeshed in DON and training and educating them in DON's techniques, models and philosophy"* (italics added). And of the Ph.D.s awarded to students from DON, all have been confined within the methodological paradigm of factor analysis and linear space. Indeed, only one of Rummel's students has questioned either part of the inner core: Phillips (1970) suggested that behavior causes behavior.

This is not to say that Rummel required a doctoral student to be within paradigm; nevertheless, it did work out this way. No doubt the acceptance or otherwise of a paradigm can be aided by the penetration of one's students into the general pool of international relations scholars. The readiness with which students from DON are accepted in other schools will surely be one indicator of the willingness of the profession to consider the relevancy of the paradigm.

In summary, we see that Rummel has acted as a sophisticated falsificationist in the Lakatos sense in his development of DON: designing and carrying out a progressive problem shift program, while hanging steadfastly to the linear algebra paradigm. Although the development of the research has been considered logical, the core of the program is not generally accepted and has thus attracted much negative comment, particularly in view of the amount of money spent on DON. When put under this pressure, Rummel points to the testing of the protective belt of middle-range hypotheses. He thus argues as a naif falsificationist—stating that field theory is a theory (rather than just a description) because it is refutable, and shows that Model 1 was in fact rejected because of confrontation with the data.

This is exactly what Lakatos would predict that the sophisticated falsificationist must do. The diversion of attention away from the inner core and toward the expendable sacrificial protective belt is vital. Undoubtedly, this action will create further hostility, but this is the only logical way that one can proceed if one is not to bury every theory beneath a mountain of anomalies.

NOTES

1. For example, the following works by Rummel would provide basic readings for those interested in field theory: "A Field Theory of Social Action with Application to Conflict within Nations," *General Systems Year Book* 10, 1965, p. 183; "Field Theory and Indicators of International Behavior," Research Report 29, July 1969; "Field and Attribute Theories of Nation Behavior: Some Mathematical Relationships," Research Report 31, August, 1969; "Social Time and International Relations," Research Report 40, June, 1970; "U.S. Foreign Relations: Conflict, Cooperation and Attribute Distances," Research Report 41, June, 1970; also see Rummel, R. J. and R. Van Atta, "Testing Field Theory on the 1963 Behavior Space of Nations," Research Report 43, August, 1970.

Inquiries regarding the research reports should be addressed to : DON Project, 2500 Campus Road, Honolulu, Hawaii 96822.

REFERENCES

ALKER, H. A. and R. SNYDER (1970) "A review of the Stanford Studies in Conflict and Integration." (unpublished)

CATTELL, R. B. and R. L. GORSUCH (1965) "The definition and measurement of national morale and morality." J. of Social Psychology 67: 77-96.

DEUTSCH, K. (1960) "Towards and inventory of basic trends and patterns in comparative and international politics." Amer. Pol. Sci. Rev. 54 (March).

GALTUNG, J. (1964) "A structural theory of aggression." J. of Peace Research 2: 95-119.

GLEDITSCH, N. P. (1970) "Rank theory, field theory and attribute theory: three approaches to interaction in the international system." DON Research Report 47. Univ. of Hawaii.

HANSON, N. R. (1958) Patterns of Discovery. Cambridge, Eng.: Cambridge Univ. Press.

HEMPEL, C. G. (1965) Aspects of Scientific Explanation. New York: Free Press.

HILTON, G. T. (1972) "Causal inference analysis: a seductive process." Admin. Sci. Q. 17: 44-54.

--- (1971) A Review of the Dimensionality of Nations Project. London: Richardson Institute for Conflict and Peace Research.

--- (1970) "The 1914 crisis: a re-assessment of the evidence and some further thoughts." Peace Research Society International Papers 13.

--- (1969) "A study of threat systems—the 1914 case." Ph.D. dissertation. University of Lancaster.

KUHN, T. S. (1962) The Structure of Scientific Revolutions. Chicago: Univ. of Chicago Press.

LAKATOS, C. and A. MUSGRAVE (1970) Criticism and the Growth of Knowledge. Cambridge, Eng.: Cambridge Univ. Press.

McCORMICK, D. (1969) "A field theory of dynamic international processes." DON Research Report 30. Univ. of Hawaii.

PARK, T. W. (1972) "The role of distance in international relations: a new look at social field theory." Behavioral Sci. 17 (July): 337-348.

--- (1969) "Asian conflict in systematic perspective: application of field theory (1955 and 1963)." DON Research Report 35. Univ. of Hawaii.

PHILLIPS, W. (1970) "A mathematical theory of conflict dynamics." DON Research Report 39. Univ. of Hawaii.

--- and R. J. RUMMEL (1969) "Forecasting international relations: some view on the relevancy of the DON project to policy planning." DON Research Report 36. Univ. of Hawaii.

RHEE, S. W. (1972) "China's cooperation, conflict and interaction behavior; viewed from Rummel's status-field theoretic perspective." DON Research Report 62. Univ. of Hawaii.

--- (1971) "Communist China's foreign behavior: an application of field theory model II." DON Research Report 57. Univ. of Hawaii.

ROSENAU, J. (1966) "Pre-theories and theories of foreign policy," in R. B. Farrell (ed.) Approaches to Comparative and International Politics. Evanston, Ill.: Northwestern Univ. Press.

RUMMELL, R. J. (1972) The Dimensions of Nations. Los Angeles: Sage Pubns.

--- (1971) "Status-field theory and international relations." DON Research Report 50. Univ. of Hawaii.

--- (1970a) "US foreign relations: conflict, cooperation, and attribute distances." DON Research Report 41. Univ. of Hawaii.

--- (1970b) "Social time and international relations." DON Research Report 40. Univ. of Hawaii.

--- (1970c) Applied Factor Analysis. Evanston: Northwestern Univ. Press.

--- (1969a) "Some empirical findings on nations and their behavior." World Politics 21 (January).

––– (1969b) "Field Theory and indicators of international behavior." DON Research Report 29. Univ. of Hawaii.

––– (1968) "Attribute and behavioral spaces of nations: variables and samples for 1950." DON Research Report 13. Univ. of Hawaii.

––– (1967a) "DON Project: a five-year program." DON Research Report 9. Univ. of Hawaii.

––– (1967b) "Understanding factor analysis." J. of Conflict Resolution 11, 4.

––– (1965a) "A field theory of social action with application to conflict within nations." General Systems Year Book 10: 183.

––– (1965b) "A social field theory of foreign conflict behavior." Peace Research Society 4.

––– and R. VAN ATTA (1970) "Testing field theory on the 1963 behavior space of nations." DON Research Report 43. Univ. of Hawaii.

RUMMEL, R. J. and C. WALL (1969) "Estimating missing data." DON Research Report 20. Univ. of Hawaii.

VINCENT, J. E. (1972) "Comments on social field theory." DON Research Report 58. Univ. of Hawaii.

WRIGHT, Q. (1955) The Study of International relations. New York: Appleton-Century-Crofts.

APPENDIX

DON RESEARCH REPORTS

1. Rummel, R. J. "Some Attributes and Behavioral Patterns of Nations." July 1966

2. ——— "Dimensions of Dyadic War—1820-1952." See *Journal of Peace Research*, August 1966

3. ——— "Dyadic Study Second Revised Variable List." August 1966

4. ——— "International Pattern and Nation Profile Delineation." April 1966

5. ——— "Attribute Space of Nations for 1963 Variable List." October 1966

6. ——— "Regional Correlations with Dimensions of Nations."

7. ——— "Understanding Factor Analysis." See *Applied Factor Analysis*, Northwestern University Press, 1970

8. ——— "Measures of International Relations." May 1967. See Article No. 11.

9. ——— "DON Project: A Five-Year Program." 1967

10. ——— "Some Empirical Findings on Nations and Their Behavior."

11. Hannah, Herbert. "Some Dimensions of International Conflict Settlement Procedures and Outcomes." February 1968

12. Hall, Dennis and R. J. Rummel. "The Patterns of Dyadic Foreign Conflict Behavior for 1963." June 1968

13. Rummel, R. J. "Attribute and Behavioral Spaces of Nations: Variables and Samples for 1950." August 1968

14. Hall, Dennis. "Computer Program Profile." June 1968

15. Phillips, Warren R. "Investigations into Alternative Techniques for Developing Empirical Taxonomies: The Results of Two Plasmodes." October 1968

16. Hall, Dennis and R. J. Rummel. "The Dynamics of Dyadic Foreign Conflict Behavior 1955 to 1963." January 1969

17. Phillips, Warren R. "Dynamic Patterns of International Conflict: A Dyadic Research Design." Ph.D. Proposal, September 1968. See Research Report No. 33.

18. Phillips, Warren R. and Dennis Hall. "Importance of Governmental Structure as a Taxonomic Scheme of Nations." See Article No. 13.

19. Park, Tong Whan. "Asian Conflict—Systematic Perspective: Application of Field Theory (1955 and 1963)." Ph.D. dissertation proposal. See Research Report No. 35.

20. Wall, Charles and R. J. Rummel. "Estimating Missing Data." January 1969

21. Pratt, R. and R. J. Rummel. "Issue Dimensions in the 1963 U.N. General Assembly." March 1969

22. Oliva, Gary and R. J. Rummel. "Foreign Conflict Patterns and Types for 1963." April 1969

23. Firestone, Joseph. "Concept Formation, System Analysis and Factor Analysis in Political Science." May 1969

24. ——— and David McCormick. "An Exploration in System Analysis of Domestic Conflict." May 1969

25. Firestone, Joseph and Gary Oliva. "National Motives and National Attributes: A Crosstime Analysis." May 1969

26. Firestone, Joseph. "National Motives and Domestic Planned Violence. An Examination of Time-lagged Correlational Trends in Cross Time Regressions." May 1969

27. Keim, Willard and R. J. Rummel. "Dynamic Patterns of Nation Conflict 1955 to 1963." June 1969

28. Rummel, R. J. "Forecasting International Relations: A Proposed Investigation of Three Mode Factor Analysis." July 1969. See Article No. 12.

29. ——— "Field Theory and Indicators of International Behavior." July 1969

30. McCormick, David. "A Field Theory of Dynamic International Processes." September 1969

31. Rummel, R. J. "Field and Attribute Theories of Nation Behavior: Some Mathematical Interrelationships." August 1969

32. Park, Tong Whan. "Peaceful Interactions in Asia: The Delineation of Nation Groups." October 1969

33. Phillips, Warren R. "Dynamic Patterns of International Conflict." October 1969

34. Rummel, R. J. "The DON Project: Policy Relevance and Overview." October 1969

35. Park, Tong Whan. "Asian Conflict in Systematic Perspective: Application of Field Theory (1965 and 1963). December 1969

36. Phillips, Warren R. and R. J. Rummel. "Forecasting International Relations: Some View on the Relevancy of the Dimensionality of Nations Project to Policy Planning." November 1969

37. Chadwick, Richard. "Notes and Tests of the Magnitude Aspect of Dyadic Behavior Predictions in Rummel's Field Theory." December 1972

38. Phillips, Warren R. "Research Proposal Submitted to the Arms Control and Disarmament Agency." June 1970

39. ——— "A Mathematical Theory of Conflict Dynamics." June 1970

40. Rummel, R. J. "Social Time and International Relations." June 1970

41. ——— "U.S. Foreign Relations: Conflict, Cooperation, and Attribute Distances." June 1970

42. Phillips, Warren R. "The Conflict Environment of Nations: A Study of Conflict Inputs to Nations in 1963." August 1970

43. Van Atta, Richard and R. J. Rummel. "Testing Field Theory on the 1963 Behavior Space of Nations." August 1970

44. Rummel, R. J. "Field Theory and the 1963 Behavior Space of Nations." August 1970

45. Park, Tong Whan. "Measuring Dynamic Patterns of Development: The Case of Asia, 1949-1968." August 1970

46. Phillips, Warren R. "International Communications." September 1970

47. Gleditsch, Nils Petter. "Rank Theory, Field Theory, and Attribute Theory: Three Approaches to Interaction in the International System." October 1970

48. Rhee, Sang Woo. "Communist China's Foreign Behavior: An Application of Field Theory Model II." August 1970

49. Phillips, Warren R. "The Dynamics of Behavioral Conflict." October 1970

50. Rummel, R. J. "Status Field Theory and International Relations." August 1971

51. Kent, George. "Policy Analysis for Action Recommendations," January 1971

52. Vincent, Jack. "Testing Some Hypotheses About Delegate Attitudes at the United Nations." April 1971

53. Wall, Charles and Alan C.H. Kam. "DYNA: Dynamic Storage and Allocation in Fortran for the IBM/360 Operating System." April 1971

54. Vincent, Jack. "An Examination of Voting Patterns in the 23rd and 24th Sessions of the General Assembly." March 1971

55. Kent, George. "The Evaluation of Policy Alternatives." March 1971

56. ——— "Teaching Practical Policy Analysis." April 1971

57. Rhee, Sang Woo. "Communist China's Foreign Behavior: An Application of Field Theory Model II." July 1971

58. Vincent, Jack. "Comments on Social Field Theory." January 1972

59. Kent, George. "Prescribing Foreign Policy." January 1972

60. ——— "Plan for Designing the Future." January 1972

61. Rhee, Sang Woo. "China's Cooperation, Conflict and Interaction Behavior; Viewed from Rummel's Status-Field Theoretic Perspective." April 1972

62. Wall, Charles. "Code Φ 991 Procedure." May 1972

63. Kent, George. "Political Design." July 1972

ARTICLES

1. Rummel, R. J. "Dimensions of Conflict Behavior Within and Between Nations," *General Systems Yearbook* 8 (1963): 1-50.

2. ——— "Testing Some Possible Predictors of Conflict Behavior Within and Between Nations," *Peace Research Society Papers,* 1964.

3. ——— "A Field Theory of Social Action with Application to Conflict Within Nations," *Yearbook of the Society for General Systems* 10 (1965).

4. ——— "A Social Field Theory of Foreign Conflict," *Peace Research Society,* Cracow Conference Papers 4 (1965).

5. ——— "A Foreign Conflict Code Sheet," *World Politics,* January 1966.

6. ——— "Dimensions of Domestic Conflict Behavior, 1946-59," *Journal of Conflict Resolution,* March 1966.

7. ——— "The Dimensionality of Nations Project," in R. Merritt and S. Rokkan (eds.), *Comparing Nations,* Yale University Press, 1966.

8. ——— "Some Dimensions in the Foreign Behavior of Nations," *Journal of Peace Research,* 3 (1966).

9. ——— "Some Attribute and Behavioral Patterns of Nations," *Journal of Peace Research,* 4 (1966).

10. ——— "Domestic Attributes and Foreign Conflict," in J. D. Singer, *Quantitative International Politics,* 1967.

11. ——— "Dimensions of Dyadic War, 1820-1952," *Journal of Conflict Resolution,* June 1967.

12. ——— "Understanding Factor Analysis," *Journal of Conflict Resolution,* December 1967.

13. ——— "Future Research on the Asian System," *East-West Center Review,* December 1967.

14. ——— "Delineating International Patterns and Profiles," *The Computer and the Policy Making Community,* 1968.

15. ——— "Progress in Understanding International Relations: The DON Project," *East-West Center Review,* March 1968.

16. ——— "Some Empirical Findings on Nations," *World Politics,* January 1969.

17. ——— "Indicators of Cross-National and International Patterns," *American Political Science Review,* March 1969.

18. ——— "Dimensions of Foreign and Domestic Conflict Behavior: A Review of Empirical Findings," in D. G. Pruitt and R. C. Snyder, *Theory and Research on the Causes of War,* 1969.

19. ——— "Forecasting International Relations: A Proposed Investigation of Three Mode Factor Analysis," *Technological Forecasting,* 1969.

20. ——— "Field and Attribute Theories of Nation Behavior: Some Mathematical Interrelationships," *Peace Research Society Papers,* Tokyo Conference, 1969 (forthcoming).

21. ——— "Dimensions of Error in Cross-National Data," in R. Naroll and R. Cohen, *Handbook of Method in Cultural Anthropology,* 1969.

22. ——— "Social Time and International Relations," *General Systems Yearbook* 17 (1972).

23. ——— "US Foreign Relations: Conflict, Cooperation, and Attribute Distances," in B. M. Russett (ed.), *Peace, War and Numbers,* Sage Pubns., 1972.

GORDON T. HILTON holds a B.A. degree from the University of Aston (Birmingham, England); and an M.S. in operations research and a Ph.D. in conflict studies (Department of Politics)—both from Lancaster University. He was Research Administrator, then Deputy Director, of the Richardson Institute for Conflict and Peace Research, London, during the period 1969-1972. Following a number of visiting lectureships in Germany and England, he is presently Assistant Professor of Political Science at Northwestern University. In addition to articles in the Journal of Peace Research, Journal of the Royal Statistical Society, *and* Administrative Science Quarterly, *his book—*Crisis and Content*—is forthcoming from English University Press. His current research continues to reflect his interests in both conflict studies and methodology: he is now processing 1,200 interviews regarding the Fleming-Walloon conflict from respondents in Brussels.*